MARCUS DALY'S

—— ROAD TO ——

MONTANA

MARCUS DALY'S
── ROAD TO ──
MONTANA

BRENDA WAHLER

THE
History
PRESS

Published by The History Press
Charleston, SC
www.historypress.com

First published 2023

Charts and maps by the author.

Manufactured in the United States

ISBN 9781467153591

Library of Congress Control Number: 2022948303

To Eric

Marcus Daly, 1895. *MHS 941-879.*

CONTENTS

PREFACE

Marcus Daly (1841–1900) developed the copper mines of Butte, Montana, into the resource that literally electrified America. From his first trip to Butte in 1876 until his death in 1900, the press eagerly followed his every move as he grew from a mine superintendent to a corporate giant.

Daly's tale is one of the genuine rags to riches stories of American capitalism, and a comprehensive biography is long overdue. There are excellent studies of Butte and the role of the Anaconda Copper Company in Montana history, but all gloss over Daly's early years. *The Dictionary of American Biography* describes the few books solely dedicated to him as "undocumented and uncritical." Their mythic elements and inaccuracies present a challenge for modern researchers.

Daly hid in plain sight. He rarely spoke of his early years and kept many secrets. His wife, Margaret, burned his business papers upon his death and destroyed their private letters before she died. Many of his colleagues did the same, turning priceless primary source materials into ashes.

There is one scholarly biography of Daly, that of K. Ross Toole (1920–1981). For his 1948 master's thesis, he was able to interview key people who were still alive, including Daly's lawyer and friend William Scallon, Daly's daughter Mary "Molly" Daly Gerard, and Katherine Evans Wellcome, the daughter of Morgan Evans, whom Daly declared to be the actual founder of Anaconda, Montana. Toole followed up this work in 1954 with a comprehensive doctoral thesis on the Anaconda Company with much material on Daly.

Another biographer who tackled Daly's life was an amateur historian from Hamilton, Montana, Ada Powell (1936–2012). Armed with a high school education and a love of the area, Powell launched an extensive study. Her self-published *Dalys of the Bitter Root* and its sequel, *Copper, Green, and Silver*, are imperfect but valuable social histories of Marcus Daly and his family. Powell was the first to recognize that Daly's story was incomplete without understanding his deep commitment to horses and the turf. He did not merely imitate his rich and powerful contemporaries. His horse ranch, the Bitter Root Stock Farm, was the expression of his life's true passion.

Toole acknowledged his frustration with the dearth of materials on Daly's early years. He provided what he had "in the hope that subsequent research may one day fill the gaps."[1]

Thus, most material about Daly is gleaned from indirect evidence, save for one group of records: those of the Bitter Root Stock Farm, where annual catalogues and carefully maintained stud books were preserved. The turf is where the secretive Daly was revealed. Normally a man who played his cards close, he socialized in the owner's boxes and betting pools. He spoke openly to the racing press, talking up his horses, his hopes, his dreams—and at times, his disappointments.

Something about horses motivates a subset of highly competitive, profit-driven people to deliberately lose money. Being a businessman, Daly publicly professed that he bred and raced horses as a moneymaking proposition, even though those in the horse business know the entire industry is a gamble and profits are rare.[2] But Daly was a gambler. He took bold risks in business and at the track. He won at both.

In my previous book, *Montana Horse Racing: A History*, Daly stepped from the shadows of the Anaconda Copper Company and demanded I devote nearly two chapters to his horse racing passion. I suppose this was no surprise. In life, he played a long game and often struck without warning—it stands to reason he waited 120 years to ambush an unsuspecting author.

This book originally intended to interweave tales of the turf with Daly's business and political life from the 1880s until his death in 1900. But instead, as I gathered the scant scraps and snippets of his early life, I wound up describing Daly's first forty years of struggle. These things happen to writers. Being an Irishman, Daly would no doubt acknowledge the role of the Pooka, the trickster, as it grabbed the narrative and galloped off in an unexpected direction.

The work before you, by necessity, is filled with hypotheses and speculation, describing Daly's road to Montana more than the man himself. But in doing so, I hope it fills some gaps. The next book in this series will examine Marcus Daly's life from 1883 to 1900, as he built two empires: one of copper and the other on the turf.

—Brenda Wahler, August 2022

Abbreviations and Notes

Modern Irish spelling is used for most Irish/Gaelic words, though some concepts use classic Irish. Monetary conversions to current value are from MeasuringWorth.com. The most conservative estimates are given in most cases.

The abbreviations used in captions and citations are as follows:

Bancroft: Bancroft Library, University of California, Berkeley
BSB: Butte-Silver Bow Public Archives
Daly Mansion: Daly Mansion Preservation Trust
LOC: Library of Congress
MHS: Montana Historical Society
NYPL: New York Public Library

ACKNOWLEDGEMENTS

Many people helped me with this project and have my thanks. All mistakes are my own, and I ask forgiveness from anyone whose advice I did not take or whom I omitted from the list below!

This project was supported by the Friends of the Butte-Silver Bow Public Archives through their Carrie Johnson Fellowship. Special thanks go to the amazing staff, board members, and volunteers at the archives, especially Ellen Crain, Aubrey Jaap, Kim Kohn, and Dianna Porter. My deepest thanks also to the Daly Mansion Preservation Trust, its board members, "history mystery" team, and Executive Director Darlene Gould for their significant in-kind support of this project. I could not have completed this book without the resources and cooperation of the University of Montana's K. Ross Toole Archives and Special Collections at the Mansfield Library, the Montana Historical Society, and the Clerks of District Court and Clerk and Recorder Offices of the Anaconda-Deer Lodge, Butte-Silver Bow, and Ravalli Counties.

Other thank-yous go to Anaconda's Copper Village Museum, the California, Nevada, and Utah State Historical Societies, the Federal District Court of Utah, the Park City Historical Society, and the Haggin Museum of Stockton, California. Most of all, my gratitude goes out to the following individuals—a list that is surely incomplete: David Armstrong, Fr. Patrick Beretta, the Bessenyey family, Patty Briggs, Kevin Daly, Rosemary Daly Marcuss, Savina Donohoe, Tony Dunne, David Emmons, Darrell Ehrlick, Richard Gibson, Larry Hoffman, Maureen "Mo" Lischke, Dawn Lynn,

Concepta McGovern, Daniel Melia, Edward Owen Teggin, Mary O'Reilly and Gerry Reilly, Ken Robison, Kate Sheehy, Victoria Short, and as always, my family, who endure my multiple rough drafts and creative quandaries.

Thanks also to The History Press for their patience as this project went through nearly as many variants as the COVID-19 virus that lurked in the background of the entire process.

THE STATUES

Daly is a born leader of men, and had opportunity been given him, he would have made his mark at court, or in the senate, or on the battlefield.
—P.A. O'Farrell[3]

On September 2, 1907—Labor Day—a heroic-scale bronze statue of Marcus Daly by sculptor Augustus St. Gaudens was dedicated in Butte, Montana. A scant seven years after his death, the canvas dropped, and Daly's fierce gaze once again looked upon the mining city, known as "the Richest Hill on Earth." With suit jacket unbuttoned, coat flung over his arm, hat in his hand, the Copper King stood with impatient energy, watching the world around him, ready to make yet another incisive decision. Behind the scenes, donations from Butte's miners, whose labor—and lives—made Daly's fortune possible, had helped immortalize the founder of the Anaconda Copper Company.[4]

In 1894, journalist P.A. O'Farrell described Daly as a "prince of the American turf and mining king of the world."[5] But Butte's people knew Daly was shaped by the challenges he faced in his earlier life. At root, he was a survivor. His youth was haunted by the Great Famine. He spent his adolescence on the riot-plagued streets of greater New York. His higher education was hands-on in the dangerous, lawless world that characterized America's western mining camps.

As Daly rose to prominence, he "made a noise" as he built his copper empire.[6] Yet he quietly challenged the Gilded Age model of a heartless

Unveiling the Daly statue, 1907. *BSB.*

robber baron. Though he joined the elite and chose to survive in the vicious world of laissez-faire capitalism, he never forgot his early years of struggle.

The people of Butte knew where he came from: amid the cheers and speeches at the statue dedication, an anonymous old-timer grumbled in an Irish brogue, "Arrah! They should have put him astride a big phite harse [*sic*]. Marcus was always wild about harses!" Others later complained of the monument's placement on narrow North Main Street, facing away from Butte's headframes. A miner named Matty Kiely insisted, "Marcus Daly never turned his arse on the mines of Butte or the miners who dug them."[7]

Daly revealed his heart when spending his discretionary dollars: he sympathized with Irish revolutionaries, even funding certain causes. His "copper, green, and silver" racing silks proudly evoked the Irish "tricolour" on tracks from California to New York. His Bitter Root Stock Farm, holding well over $1 million worth of pedigreed animals, was one of the finest horse ranches in the United States.[8] In the mines and on the turf, Daly was a "plunger," a gambler who took risks and moved boldly.

The people of Butte and Anaconda worried when he took the Anaconda Company public in 1895, but he reassured them: "My home is in Montana," he said, "my interests are here. My friends—I have any man's share of them—are here, and I have no other plan in the world except to stay with them."[9]

In April 1899, the people truly feared Daly had forgotten them when he became president of the newly formed Amalgamated Copper Company—they did not realize he was a dying man.* The renal failure and hypertension that killed him in November 1900 was called Bright's disease, a descriptor that now covers several possible conditions, including untreated type II diabetes.[10]

In death, the people forgave Daly. On November 15, 1900, the day of Daly's funeral in New York City, Butte and Anaconda shut down their mines,

---

* "The Company" went through multiple rounds of corporate restructuring and renaming. Amalgamated Copper was formed in 1899 by a reorganization of the Anaconda Copper Company. In 1915, it returned to the name Anaconda Copper.

Marcus Daly statue in original location, 1939. *LOC.*

shops, and reduction works so local citizens could also pay their respects. Father Callahan of Butte presided over a requiem mass, describing Daly as "one who, though affluent and all powerful, was best known, not in the gilded palaces of the rich, nor in the circles of those seeking high places, but in the homes of the poor and the afflicted and the downtrodden."[11]

By 1907, as the Company tightened its ruthless "Copper Collar" of monopoly and power, the people of Butte sought a legendary hero. They wanted—and needed—to remember a leader who cared about them.

Daly was an imperfect hero. He was known to Montanans for his driving energy, magnetism, charm, and charity, but also for his hot temper, sarcasm that could "peel the bark from a tree," and ability to tenaciously hold a grudge. Though described by K. Ross Toole as "a restless man and a doer of things," Daly played a long game and adeptly hid his motives from his opponents until it was time to strike. In a battle for supremacy with his fellow Copper Kings—his implacable enemy W.A. Clark and the brash upstart Frederick Augustus Heinze—he blatantly manipulated the economy and politics of Montana.[12]

Daly earned many of his accolades. His generosity was notable for an individual of his wealth and power. He disliked the label "Copper King" and tended to put others forward while he maneuvered behind the scenes.[13] In contrast, Daly's enemies argued that his every action was manipulative, his temper "violent," and W.A. Clark once bitterly declared, "When Daly cannot rule, he tries to ruin."[14]

But ultimately, Daly got the statue—and became more myth than man. He differed from the other Copper Kings on a crucial point: he blended leadership with responsibility and built communities. Knowingly or otherwise, he accepted the role of "boss Irishman," a descendant of the *ceann fine*, the historic local chieftains of Ireland.

Daly offered Butte as a place with homes and jobs for the Emerald Isle diaspora and succeeded beyond even his wildest imagining. By 1900, a quarter of Butte's population was Irish. Some émigrés recounted tales that Daly greeted them in person as they wearily descended the steps of a passenger train, having arranged a place for them to live or providing them a few basic goods.[15]

The people remembered that when miners died at work—sadly frequent events—Daly saw to it that their widows had a home and their sons a job. When men were disabled—also far too common—he provided simpler work "that would not overtax their strengths." They remembered his death in November 1900 and how the destitute soon suffered the winter cold because he was no longer there to say, "Deliver to the poor of Butte three hundred tons of coal."[16]

A figure struck down in his prime—Daly was fifty-eight when he died—fit an archetype from ancient Éire's mythic golden days: a hero, bold and brave, flawed and tragic. It did not matter that Daly died a humble death in bed. The people wanted to remember that he fought the good fight for them while he was alive. After he died, a comparison between the historic British domination of Ireland and the Company's domination of Montana was all too apt.

It is hard to say how Daly might have felt about his statue. He personally worked to promote another Irishman as Montana's hero, and in 1898 became president of the Thomas Francis Meagher Memorial Association.[17] The Meagher project continued after Daly's death, and in 1905, a statue of the Irish revolutionary and Montana territorial governor—astride a great bronze horse—was unveiled on the front lawn of the state capitol building in Helena.

In Daly's lifetime, Butte became home to immigrants from around the world, but this American haven was also a hell of sorts. Copper ore in Butte was treated by heap roasting. Starting in 1880, the mining companies layered stacks of copper ore and wood, set it aflame, and soon, the impurities in the ore ignited in a self-sustaining inferno that burned for weeks, spewing sulfur and arsenic into the sky. The roasting stacks killed trees and grass for miles around, claiming human deaths as well. In 1889, W.A. Clark made facetious excuses to continue the process, stating, "It has been believed by all the physicians of Butte that the smoke that sometimes prevails there is a disinfectant and destroys the microbes that constitute the germs of disease."[18]

Daly took a run at creating something better. In 1883, he built a copper refining operation and a town, Anaconda, twenty-five miles west of Butte. Tall smokestacks directed smoke elsewhere, and residents breathed easier. Future generations faced environmental consequences downwind and downstream, but in Daly's lifetime, Anaconda's "Old Works" were an improvement that also brought copper refining in-house and under his control. Though profit-driven, Daly's actions still spoke volumes. He moved his own family to Anaconda and declared it his legal residence for the rest of his life.[19]

In 1886, at the foot of the Bitterroot Range, Daly created his vision of heaven: the Bitter Root Stock Farm. There, he traded the heat of the mines and stench of smelters for cool breezes, grazing horses, and the shade of trees reminiscent of his home in County Cavan. This Eden was still practical: he

Horses with Keeper, Marcus Daly Bitterroot Farm. Henry Cross, 1892.

The Daly statue overlooking Butte from the campus of Montana Tech. The white object on top of the mountain ridge is Our Lady of the Rockies. *Wahler.*

ran cattle, grew irrigated crops, and built the nearby town of Hamilton to support the lumber mill that supplied timber to his mines.

His life is revealed in the biblical adage, "For where your treasure is, there will your heart be also."[20] Daly's treasure went into new communities and his magnificent Thoroughbreds. Anaconda and Hamilton became far more than mere company towns. Daly supported charities and entrepreneurs as they built schools and hospitals, pharmacies and banks, hotels, theaters—and racetracks.

In 1941, the old-timers were mollified when Daly's monument was moved to the entrance of the Montana School of Mines (now Montana Technological University, popularly called Montana Tech), overlooking Butte. The *Montana Standard* declared, "There, it will give to most of us who honor the memory of Marcus Daly a clearer idea of this great man who surmounted so many obstacles, scoffed at so many discouragements, refused to permit his faith to waver when others were disheartened."[21]

Today, Daly's statue gazes on the city he helped build—and what came after. The regal 1910 county courthouse sits on land that once held his family home, but the Granite Mountain memorial up the hill recalls the 168 deaths resulting from the Speculator Mine disaster of 1917.[22] The Berkeley pit, started in 1955, devoured Daly's Anaconda mine and all its works on its way to becoming part of the largest Superfund site in the United States. Still, "Butte, America" remains vibrant and proud, over 150 years after its start as a struggling mining camp.

Across the valley from Daly's statue, at the top of the Continental Divide, sits *Our Lady of the Rockies*, a ninety-foot-tall statue of the Virgin Mary designed and built by the people of Butte. Installed in 1985, *Our Lady* gave hope to a community decimated in the 1980s, when Atlantic Richfield Company, successor to Anaconda Copper, shut down the mines, pumps, and smelters in Butte, Anaconda, and Great Falls.[23] As these two monuments regard one another, sacred and secular, peaceful and—at times—profane, each define the complicated mix that shaped both Daly's road to Montana and the American West itself: heaven and hell; idealism and exploitation; big dreams and unintended consequences.

PART I

STRUGGLING YOUTH

1

COUNTY CAVAN

Marcus Daly was born on December 5, 1841. His parents, Luke and Mary Coyle Daly, lived in Derrylea, a townland in Crosserlough Parish, southwest of the market town of Ballyjamesduff in County Cavan, Ulster Province, Ireland.[24] Daly lived there until 1856, when he immigrated to America.

Most accounts of Daly's life state that he was one of eleven children. Seven, including Daly, reached America. His oldest sister, Anna, preceded him. Five younger siblings followed: Thomas, Patrick, Mary, Owen, and Katherine (known as "Kate"). Anna, Patrick, and Kate ultimately joined Daly in Montana, where Patrick became a Montana state senator. Mary, Owen, and Thomas settled in the greater New York area. At least four other siblings remained in Ireland; the 1911 Irish census listed unmarried siblings Luke and Honor Daly sharing a house in Derrylea. In the 1901 census, a brother, James, was also recorded as living with them. Crosserlough baptism and cemetery records identify a brother named Peter, who died in early adulthood.[25]

Luke Daly was listed as a tenant farmer in 1856 and probably was one throughout his life—few Irish Catholics were landowners. Though the 1837 *Topographical Dictionary of Ireland* noted some of the Connacht coal field was in northwest Cavan, and in 1854, a small, short-lived coal mine opened about twenty miles west of Ballyjamesduff, there is no evidence to date that the family had any connection to the mining industry.[26]

Little else is known about Daly's youth; records are scarce, and he seldom discussed his early years. Beyond the bare facts are stories that may never be independently verified. There are claims his family was "comfortable," while

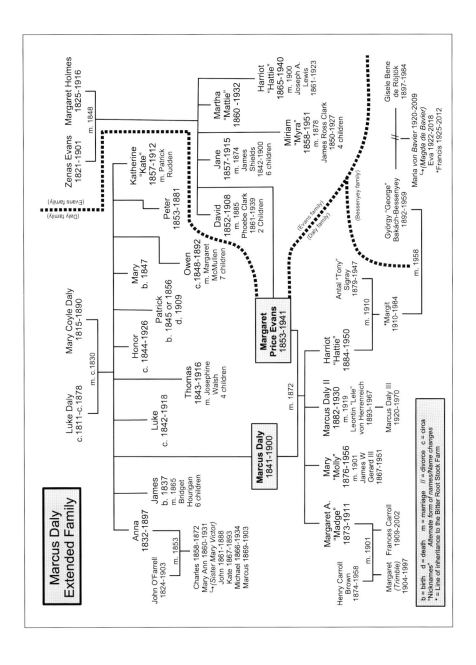

Mountnugent Bridge, County Cavan. The nearby village of Mountnugent was once known as Dalysbridge. *Brenda Montgomery.*

others say they were destitute. Similarly, when Daly left Ireland for America, some accounts paint him as a lone figure in a cruel world, yet the evidence suggests he had a rich network of family and friends.

What is known is the public pride Daly took in his Irish heritage. It went beyond the tricolour racing silks he placed on his jockeys. He put time and money into nationalist causes and gave jobs to his fellow Irish expatriates as soon as he had the power to hire. He sent remittances home to his family and gave funds to Crosserlough Parish, where his mother and one of his brothers were buried.[27]

Forming a picture of the young boy in Cavan starts with the world that shaped him. Biographer Isaac Marcosson described Daly as "a child of peat and bog."[28] This fits, as County Cavan is a beautiful landlocked region of lakes and lush green hills. In 1912, Ballyjamesduff (in Irish, *Baile Shéamais Dhuibh*) was idealized in song:

> *The Garden of Eden has vanished, they say*
> *But I know the lie of it still;*
> *Just turn to the left at the bridge of Finea*
> *And stop when halfway to Cootehill.*

'Tis there I will find it,
I know sure enough
When fortune has come to me call,
Oh the grass it is green around Ballyjamesduff
And the blue sky is over it all.

—Percy French, "Come Back, Paddy Reilly, to Ballyjamesduff"

A White Horse

When the old-timer in Butte said Daly's statute should have included a "phite harse," he tapped ancient archetypes. Though Luke and Mary Daly baptized their children in the Catholic faith, Éire's ancient paganism remained visible in Ulster. Today, the Cavan County Museum in Ballyjamesduff preserves the Killycluggin Stone, which represents Crom Crúaich, a god allegedly overthrown by Saint Patrick.[29]

Perhaps Daly's supporters envisioned him on a steed that carried gods: Énbarr, swifter than the wind, could cross both land and sea. Énbarr carried Lugh, the god of kings, who gave horses to the Irish. Ireland's ancient harvest festivals of Lúnasa honored Lugh with honor games and horse racing.[30] What better mount for the horse-loving Copper King?

But perhaps Butte's Irish pictured Daly with a hero's steed. Cú Chulainn, the son of Lugh, defended Ulster against overwhelming odds. The goddess Macha gave the bold young hero a magical chariot horse named Liath Macha, who shed tears of blood before Cú Chulainn's final battle. At the 1907 statue dedication, speaker Patrick Boland said of Daly, "No fairer or braver knight ever drew sword."[31]

Of course, a white horse was also a traditional mount that carried souls to paradise. One carried the warrior-poet Oisîn to visit Tír Na nÓg, an ageless land where everyone lived in happiness.[32]

But the old-timer might not have imagined gods and heroes at all. Perhaps, with a twinkle in his eye and tongue firmly in cheek, he thought of the trickster. The Irish told tales of the Pooka, a shapeshifter who could manifest as a horse, luring unsuspecting victims to his back and carrying them off on a wild ride.[33] Given the twists and turns of Daly's life, perhaps the capricious Pooka was his destined mount.

A LIFETIME PASSION

Horses in Ireland are a drug…The soil is of a sweet and plentiful
grass…and the hills, especially near the sea-coasts, are hard and rough,
and so fit to give them shape, and breath, and sound feet.…We see horses
bred of excellent shape, and vigour, and size.
—Sir William Temple, 1673 [34]

Beyond myth, horses were a major part of Irish culture—and possibly played a role in the livelihood of the Daly family.

According to a 1934 biography written by Hugh Daly of Butte (not a direct relative), the Luke Daly family had "more than a local reputation as horse breeders and trainers."[35] Though the work is a hagiography, the two men knew one another, and specific details like this could be accurate. Marcus Daly's passion for racehorses certainly went beyond the fashionable interest of a Gilded Age dilettante seeking to display money and power.

In an 1892 interview, Daly said that as a youth, he dreamed of owning horses. His granddaughter Margit Sigray Bessenyey, who came to own his Bitter Root Stock Farm, agreed that Daly fulfilled his childhood dream by building a horse ranch in Montana's Bitterroot Valley.[36]

Daly's Bitter Root Stock Farm, purchased in 1886, grew into a twenty-two-thousand-acre estate where his discretionary spending and heart resided. "The awful work thrown upon me by my business would kill me," he is alleged to have said, "but for the fact that now and then, I can run up to the Bitter Root and see the colts. That place has cost me a lot of money, but it is worth it to me when I stop to think of the relief it furnishes."[37]

Daly put over $1 million into the purchase of Thoroughbreds (over $26 million in 2020 dollars), and as much as $5 million into infrastructure. The Stock Farm focused on the animals' well-being, with covered training tracks, steam-heated barns, and a state-of-the-art veterinary clinic. Over 1,200 horses grazed the fields. Three specially outfitted railcars carried Daly's racehorses in livestock luxury from coast to coast.[38]

Daly's friend and Montana cattle king Conrad Kohrs observed that "Marcus Daly did a great deal of traveling [during his early years in Montana]," specifically adding, "usually on horseback or in a buggy," a comment verifying that Daly traveled light and fast and handled his own horses.[39] What is unknown is whether Daly routinely handled horses in his Irish youth or if he trudged from place to place as wagons, carriages, and riders passed him by.

Daly at the Bitter Root Stock Farm, Montana, circa 1899. *Daly Mansion.*

In any case, the man was horse obsessed—but perhaps, so are the Irish in general.

Ireland's fondness for horses is well-documented. In Cavan, the Loughanleagh Festival of Lúnasa existed for centuries. Even during England's brutal conquest, King James I still permitted a fair in 1608. That celebration, now called the Fair of Muff, is the oldest traditional horse fair in Ireland and is still held annually.[40] Derrylea is roughly twenty miles away from the fair's site near Kingscourt—a significant journey in Daly's time. But if the family bred and trained horses, they could have done business there.

Whatever connections the Daly family had to the horse world, they probably watched horse races on Market Day in Ballyjamesduff. Before and even during the Great Famine, these events presented a "day out for Irish people."[41]

Spirituality and sport were bright spots in people's everyday lives. The rest of the time, it took hard work to eke out a life of bare subsistence.

The modern Connemara pony resembles the historic native horses of Cavan. *Wikimedia Commons.*

WARS AND CONQUEST

The forces shaping Marcus Daly went back centuries, to the closely-knit Irish clans that made up the basic unit of society. Their leaders, the *ceann fine*, were local chieftains who meted out rewards and punishments, defending their clans with both diplomacy and war. Historian David Emmons described Daly and other nineteenth-century Irish American leaders as heirs to this leadership tradition.[42]

When not fighting one another, Irish clans fought repeated waves of foreign invasion. In the sixteenth and seventeenth centuries, English occupation finally expanded beyond the Pale—their longstanding core area of control—and they gained hegemony over most of Ireland. Ulster held out the longest, but in 1609, County Cavan became part of the Plantation of Ulster, a colonization scheme that brutally pacified the region by taking Irish-owned land and granting it to Scottish and English settlers. It reduced Irish Catholics to servants of their Protestant conquerors—tenants on land they once owned.[43]

Oliver Cromwell arrived in 1649. According to Hugh Daly's account, during Cromwell's reign of terror, clan Daly (originally Ó Dálaigh) scattered north and west from their homeland in County Westmeath into Connacht Province and to Ulster's Counties Cavan and Monaghan. Hugh Daly poetically claimed the Ó Dalys descended from "the princes of Corea Adaim," while Irish cultural historian Patrick Woulfe noted the Ó Dálaigh clan were chieftains in Corca Adain (or Adhaimh) in Westmeath, later known as bards and poets.[44]

The Restoration of 1660 brought temporary relief from Cromwell's brutality, but after the 1690 Battle of the Boyne, the Penal Laws were put into place. Edmund Burke declared them "as well fitted for the oppression, impoverishment and degradation of a people…as ever proceeded from the perverted ingenuity of man." From 1695 onward, Irish Catholics (and some non-Anglican Protestants) lost nearly all of their civil rights. They could not vote, teach, practice law, own weapons, intermarry with Protestants, or adopt children. Land ownership was restricted, and farm tenancy was time limited. Most clergy were banished on pain of death, and those remaining faced onerous restrictions. By 1778, only about 5 percent of Irish land remained in Catholic hands. Tenants paid rents to often-absentee landlords who could evict a family for any reason—or no reason at all.[45]

CAVAN AND THE GREAT FAMINE

After the Acts of Union of 1800, the Penal Laws were slowly repealed. By Daly's birth in 1841, priests had returned, children could attend school, and land tenure had stabilized. Still, British control remained. A young Irish Catholic absorbed historic trauma on top of personal experience and grew up believing that justice only existed outside the law and success required cunning, deception, and secrecy. By adulthood, Daly's jovial, extroverted façade masked a master of misdirection and subterfuge.[46]

Biographers debate the economic status of the Daly family. Hugh Daly said they were "comfortable," and so do oral histories told by County Cavan locals. On this point, Hugh Daly is credible; he generally preferred to describe Irish life as bleak. Sometimes styling himself Hugh Ó Daly, he was an active member of Butte's Robert Emmet Literary Association, an affiliate of the militant Irish nationalist Clan Na Gael.[47]

Other biographers believed the Dalys were poor. Isaac Marcosson called Marcus Daly "a fugitive from a poverty-haunted farm." K. Ross Toole argued that evidence of the Dalys being a well-off farm family came from photographs of a nice home Daly's sister Honor built much later, using money sent from America. Historian Michael Malone also argued that the Dalys lived a life of subsistence.[48]

An old stone outbuilding that still stands on land Luke Daly rented has mistakenly been identified as the family hovel. But according to local Cavan history, the now-vanished Luke Daly home was large, complete with a garden and an apple orchard.[49]

Most likely, the family's standard of living plummeted as the Great Famine decimated Ireland from 1845 to 1849. From a pre-famine population of 8 million, about 1.5 million people succumbed to starvation and disease. By 1851, another 1 million emigrated, including Anna Daly. Ciarán Ó Murchadha wrote that famine emigration produced "one of the greatest population displacements of modern times, an exodus on a stunning scale that has no other nineteenth-century parallel."[50]

Daly's family may have been among those fortunate enough to stay on their land. Many landlords evicted their tenants during the famine, but Catholics in nineteenth-century County Cavan had some protection. An unwritten "Tenant-right of Ulster" limited evictions as long as families paid their rents.[51]

It is unknown how the Dalys survived, but they may have raised cash crops—only potatoes suffered the blight. During the famine, Ireland was a net exporter of food, both grain and meat. Historian Cecil Woodham-Smith explained, "No issue has provoked so much anger…as the indisputable fact that huge quantities of food were exported from Ireland to England…when the people of Ireland were dying of starvation."[52]

The only known anecdote from Daly's boyhood was published in 1922. According to the story, Daly visited County Cavan after becoming a wealthy man. There, he encountered a gruff farmer named Cummings, who asked Daly if he remembered that he used to feed Cummings's pigs. Daly was said to have paused a moment and then replied, "Indeed, I do, John, and I didn't do it well!"[53]

The story, vaguely attributed to "Daly's friends," is not implausible. Oral historians from Cavan also assert that Daly visited the area as an adult. A snippet of documentation supports the story: Griffith's valuation of 1856–57 listed a "John Cummins" living in County Cavan.[54]

While Daly may have dreamed of owning horses while tending pigs, survival came first, and brutality to animals haunted everyday Irish life. During the famine, desperate people butchered decomposing livestock

Stone outbuilding on land once tenanted by Luke Daly. *Mary O'Reilly.*

Life during the Great Famine. *"Funeral at Skibbereen,"* Illustrated London News, *1847.*

carcasses and made "black pudding" from the clandestine bloodletting of live animals. People targeted by paramilitary forces saw their dogs clubbed to death, stables set on fire, and farm horses shot.[55]

Post–Great Famine

Griffith's valuation indicates Luke Daly's post-famine property allotment was larger than most. That landholding, as well as a home like Honor's, would rank the family as relatively well-off "strong farmers." Such tenants became local leaders and their homes a neighborhood gathering spot, a "céilí house," where people told stories, played music, discussed news of the day, and discreetly shared rumors of rebellion.[56]

Little is known about Daly's formal education, but in Butte, Daly spent his evenings with friends reading newspapers, and he testified before the United States Senate in 1900 that he "read the papers every morning." While he usually dictated his correspondence, that was common business practice. William Scallon said Daly did not like to write unless he had to, but documents written in Daly's own hand—legible with occasional misspellings—exist. He charmed the press with his sarcasm and word play. The verbatim transcript of Daly's Senate testimony revealed his grammar and syntax—his speech sometimes fell short of Queen Victoria's English, reflecting his Irish dialect and working-class roots.[57]

Toole alleged Daly was home-schooled by his mother, trotting out an American frontier myth inconsistent with the Irish experience. More likely, Daly attended a primary school. Irish Catholic parents valued schools, particularly because the English historically restricted them. Daly's parents had three options: a system of free national schools created in 1831, informal (at times secret) hedge schools that operated in defiance of the English for generations, and Catholic schools that grew steadily after repeal of the Penal Laws. In 1851, when Daly was a child, 4,704 schools enrolled 520,401 pupils—a majority of Irish children. That said, attendance was not compulsory, and absentee rates were high. The famine disrupted children's schooling, as did their families' need for labor.[58]

The family's politics are another area where there is much interest but little data. Hugh Daly claimed that Luke Daly was a member of the Young

Ireland independence movement and that clan Ó Dálaigh had fought English rule since the "Norman Conquest," referring to the Anglo-Norman invasion of Ireland in 1169.[59]

Given Hugh Daly's Irish nationalism, he may have been painting with broad strokes. Yet there is evidence that Marcus Daly held radical sympathies. Militant elements of the Young Ireland movement formed the Irish Republican Brotherhood (IRB), which had many American supporters. In 1865, a "Mark Daley" was on the committee for a "grand ball" in Nevada, sponsored by the IRB-affiliated Fenian Brotherhood.[60] There is no evidence Daly did more than socialize with the group, but the ball was probably a fundraiser; some Fenians attempted a military raid into Canada in 1866, and others joined Ireland's 1867 Fenian Uprising.

After becoming wealthy and powerful in Montana, Daly donated his time and money as he pleased, providing more clues to his beliefs. Daly sent $3,000 to Irish home rule advocate Charles Parnell in 1886 and donated over £500 to Parnell's Irish National League. He also hosted activist Michael Davitt during a visit to Butte that same year, even introducing Davitt at a public event. Although Daly died before the Thomas Francis Meagher statue at the Montana Capitol was completed, he led the initial fundraising effort.[61]

His expressions of Irish patriotism increased Daly's popularity with his workers. Still, Daly hedged his bets. As an example, he was nominated for membership in Butte's hotbed of Irish nationalism, the Robert Emmet Literary Association, but apparently declined the invitation, as he was never inducted.[62]

One Daly sibling who remained in Ireland was associated with militants. In 1921, Honor Daly's nice house was destroyed by a British-backed "Black and Tan" paramilitary group, because her home apparently sheltered members of the Irish Republican Army.[63]

Whether the Daly family was comfortable or impoverished, militant or not, they faced hard work and economic struggles. The challenges of Irish life especially weighed on its young, who had few opportunities to advance in life. Post-famine farmers earned more for their crops and livestock during Britain's far-off Crimean War of 1853–56. But the end of that conflict saw a drop in commodity prices without a drop in rents.[64] And thus, the Irish exodus continued.

Daly left Ireland when he was fourteen.* He was considered a man, ready to make his way in the world. He became one of the thirty-six thousand people who left County Cavan between 1851 and 1860, one among another one million Irish emigrants.[65]

---

* Most accounts state Daly left Ireland in 1856 at age fifteen, but his birthday was in December; few emigrants took ship then.

GREATER NEW YORK

Sometime in 1856, most likely in the spring, Marcus Daly boarded a ship and headed for America. He disembarked at New York City, where he remained for five critically formative adolescent years. Daly said little about his life as a teenager. His daughter Mary Daly "Molly" Gerard told historian K. Ross Toole that Daly had worked in Brooklyn, but she knew little else.[66]

One can sketch an outline by looking at the world in which he lived. Greater New York in 1856 was an amalgam of race, religion, and language where the Irish had established a beachhead. They made up almost 30 percent of New York City's population—and were a despised minority, subject to 55 percent of the city's arrests.[67]

When Daly arrived, only the lowest-paying jobs were open to a boy like him. Employment advertisements often stated, "Protestant Only" and even "No Irish Need Apply." Nativism was on the march, and the anti-immigrant, anti-Catholic American Party, known to history as the Know-Nothings, was at its zenith of power, at one point counting one hundred members of Congress and eight governors in its ranks.[68]

After making his fortune, Daly delighted in returning to New York. Once, he allegedly told some Montana locals, "Boys, I am going back there to live. I am going to buy me a silk hat and a gold-headed cane and have a splurge. I feel that I have earned one." But he reasserted loyalty to Montana upon his return, claiming, "It is fine for about three weeks."[69] Notwithstanding the tales he told his cronies, Daly visited the city repeatedly—and stayed longer

City of New York, 1856 (Castle Garden at bottom left). *LOC.*

than three weeks. By 1886, he was known well enough in New York that the satirical newspaper *Puck* included him in a cartoon.[70]

His connection to New York was lifelong. In the 1890s, Daly's Montana-raised Thoroughbreds became champions at tracks in the greater New York area. In the end, his death in 1900 occurred in his suite at Manhattan's Hotel Netherland. After an elaborate funeral at nearby St. Patrick's Cathedral, Daly's body was buried in Green-Wood Cemetery in Brooklyn.

When Daly's estate sold most of his horses, the best were shipped east. Ed Tipton of the Fasig-Tipton Sales Company, who once managed Daly's tracks in Butte and Anaconda, organized the 1901 dispersal, the greatest sale of Thoroughbred stock in America at that time, held at Madison Square Garden.[71]

THE VOYAGE

Daly's first challenge was getting to America. His sister Anna probably sent remittances to Ireland, helping her brother make the trip.[72] If Anna sent letters along with money, Daly had some idea of what to expect. There was

Daly (*top right window*) observing assorted New York figures dressed as characters from Gilbert & Sullivan's *Mikado*. *"Our Japanese Village,"* Puck, *January 13, 1886.*

broader guidance as well: in 1851, a Boston priest, Reverend J. O'Hanlon, published *The Irish Emigrant's Guide for the United States*, which offered helpful advice for travelers and described circumstances young Daly probably faced.

Daly most likely took a sailing ship. Steamships were beginning to ply the Atlantic, but they charged expensive fares beyond the means of the average traveler.

He probably took a berth in steerage, where he got a bare bunk in the hold and had to provide his own bedding. O'Hanlon noted that all ships carrying passengers were supposed to have at least five feet "between [sleeping] decks." This rule was often ignored, and spaces designed for two people often slept three. To get more breathing room, O'Hanlon advised taking a berth on larger ships, recommending the three-masted liners, which were authorized to carry six hundred passengers. He also recommended sailing on American ships, because they were built for speed and carried more cargo.[73]

O'Hanlon urged travelers to pack lightly, convert their belongings to coin and guard it well. He told families to band together on board and said single people "would do well to combine in parties of two or three" for mutual assistance.[74]

The port from which Daly embarked is not known, but it was probably Liverpool. Ships laden with freight sailed from Dublin, Belfast, and other Irish ports but with limited passenger accommodations and high fares. Most emigrants traveled to the seamy British town and booked an Atlantic crossing from there.[75]

In the 1850s, a journey to America was "seldom" longer than six weeks, but Parliament required ships leaving the British Isles to be provisioned for ten. April was considered the best month to leave, with plentiful ships and reasonable fares.[76]

By law, each fare-paying passenger on an English-flagged ship was supposed to have three quarts of water per day and a weekly ration of five pounds of potatoes or seven pounds of hard bread, biscuit, or grain. American-flagged ships had more palatable regulations, adding a pound of salt pork without bones, plus a few ounces of sugar, molasses, tea, and vinegar to the weekly allotment of bread and water. These sustenance diets were known for their poor quality, and the quantities provided were often less than advertised. Knowing this, O'Hanlon wrote an extensive grocery list for travelers to purchase ahead of time and bring on board: it included bacon, dried fish, eggs, butter, and oatmeal. He also recommended adding small luxuries such as chocolate, pepper, and mustard.

Passengers cooked their own meals at communal cook fires contained within long trench-like grates. During bad weather, fires were not allowed, and meals were eaten cold. Utensils, dishes, and soap were the passengers' responsibility, though the ships provided washing buckets. Cleanliness depended on the discipline imposed by the captain and the collective habits of the passengers. Vermin often infested berths and luggage. Disease was a constant worry.[77]

Upon a ship's arrival in New York Harbor, officials conducted an inspection to determine if any contagion had broken out on board. Passengers had to prove they were free of disease, not infirm, nor otherwise apt to become a public charge. Anyone who was seriously ill would be "detained" at the Marine Hospital grounds on Staten Island, and if necessary, an entire ship could be quarantined for thirty days. Once cleared, the next stop was the Battery at the tip of Manhattan Island. Castle Garden, a new immigrant processing center (the predecessor of Ellis Island) opened there in 1855.[78] From there, newly arrived travelers were scattered to the winds.

CITY LIFE

Hugh Daly declared that young Marcus Daly arrived in America "without money or friends." He was exaggerating. As genealogist John Grenham explained, "Nobody ever left Ireland to go to America." People traveled to join family and take promised jobs. Daly's sister Anna blazed the trail. Her obituary stated she came to America in 1851 and married John O'Farrell in Connecticut in 1853. She may have arrived earlier: the 1850 U.S. census listed "Ann Daly" of Ireland, age eighteen, living at a women's boarding house in New Haven, Connecticut.[79]

Some accounts state that Anna was in California when her brother reached America, but others suggest young Daly lived in New York with "a sister" for a time. Anna and John O'Farrell did go west first; the 1860 U.S. census found them in Placer County, California, and listed their first child, Charles, as being born in California in 1858.[80]

Whether alone or under Anna's wing, Daly probably found employment early on. The list of jobs Daly possibly held is long. Various biographers state that he sold newspapers and was later a dock worker. Some add that he was a runner for a brokerage house, delivered telegrams, and may have been promoted to telegrapher. He worked in a "Morocco" (leather tanning) factory and cared for horses as a livery hostler or as a barn hand at a racing stable.[81]

As an adult, Daly's winning, "hail fellow well met" personality got him promoted to leadership roles and endeared him to many. A teenaged Daly could no doubt quickly charm a boss into hiring him. But given he also carried a hot temper, restlessness, and a penchant for snark into adulthood, the jobs he most likely held during those crucial five years were "all of the above."

Even working diligently, the young Daly earned a pittance. By one account, he started out with wages of $2.00 a week. At most, an unskilled laborer earned $1.00 a day, working six days a week. A steerage passage to California was advertised to cost between $75.00 and $125.00, and basic needs came before saving money for ship fare. A single boy could find economy in lodging; if Daly did not live with his family, floor space to sleep with access to a bucket toilet could be had for about $0.18 a week. However, food was expensive—an 1860 analysis estimated it took between 68 and 86 percent of one's wages. Additional money went to clothing and other necessities.[82]

However destitute Daly was, a young person would have trouble saving every spare penny when there was fun to be had. The greater New York area had much to offer: Coney Island, with its beaches and racetracks, was already a recreation center in the 1850s. It was served by steamers from Manhattan Island and was reachable from Brooklyn with a twenty-six-cent fare on a horse-drawn streetcar.[83]

Described by historian Michael Malone as a "fun-loving fellow," the adolescent Daly was probably a more energetic and impulsive version of the adult, who loved gambling and horse racing, appeared at any social event of note, and was comfortable with calculated risk. Daly may have ignored elders like his sister and Father O'Hanlon, who warned against "hanging idly about the boardinghouses and taverns," with "expenses…daily accumulating, whilst…money is diminishing."[84]

A Hand Up

Notwithstanding later stories of Daly as a self-made man, he—and Irish Catholics in general—did not go it alone. O'Hanlon's guide advised new arrivals to seek out the New York Irish Emigrant Society, which managed remittances, provided charity, and gave honest information to the naïve. Most of all, the society had leads on jobs.[85]

Another source of support was the Society of St. Tammany, known to history as Tammany Hall. Despite its historic notoriety for corruption, the Tammany machine provided an economic safety net in an era when the government did not. Daly's later machinations in Montana business and politics suggest he was shaped not only by the *ceann fine* of Ireland, but also by New York's retail politics: beneficiaries of Tammany's largess "repaid" this charity by supporting Tammany candidates at the polls, creating a cycle of mutual benefit. Newly naturalized Irish voters were a key constituency.[86]

Daly arrived as New York City faced chaos and unrest. While Tammany Hall championed assistance for the poor, its cronyism was so blatant that Mayor Fernando Wood's New York Municipal Police Force was disbanded in favor of the barely less corrupt Metropolitan Police, created by Governor John King. Conflict between these two forces resulted in the Great Police Riot of June 16, 1857. While the police brawled among themselves, gangs ruled the streets. Less than three weeks after the police riot, Lower Manhattan erupted. A Catholic gang named the Dead Rabbits faced off against the anti-Irish Bowery Boys in the Five Points Riot of July 4–5, 1857, which left twelve dead and dozens injured.[87]

At their best, Tammany politicians doubled as social workers. At their worst, they had few qualms about bending the rules and using political connections for personal benefit. An example of both was a contemporary of Daly's, George Washington Plunkitt (1842–1924).

Both Daly and Plunkitt spent their New York adolescence in a world being built by the Tammany machine. Daly wound up in Montana, where he created a "machine" of his own. Plunkitt became a Tammany ward heeler who unabashedly acknowledged what he called "honest graft," declaring, "I seen my opportunities, and I took 'em." He justified his actions as the way of "men who have made big fortunes in politics."[88] But he also served his constituents.

A 1905 memoir described one day in his life. It started when the doorbell woke Plunkitt at 2 a.m. and he was asked to bail out a saloon keeper. At 6 a.m., the bell of a horse-drawn fire wagon reawakened him, and he followed it to the scene, spending two hours finding housing and clothing for the now-homeless victims. By then, the courthouse was open. Plunkitt went there, advocated for six drunks, located counsel to assist a widow, then paid the rent of a poor family to prevent their eviction and gave them a dollar for food. He returned home, spending three hours helping men find jobs. Then he attended two funerals, ran a political meeting, went to a church fair, and listened to the woes of twelve pushcart peddlers who had police trouble. He ended the day at a wedding reception and a dance before going to bed at midnight.[89]

Daly mimicked both sides of the Tammany recipe. He provided jobs and social charity but requested political loyalty in return, encouraged as needed with liquor, cash, and possibly, implicit threats.[90] When it came to business, throughout his life, Daly also "seen his opportunities and took 'em."

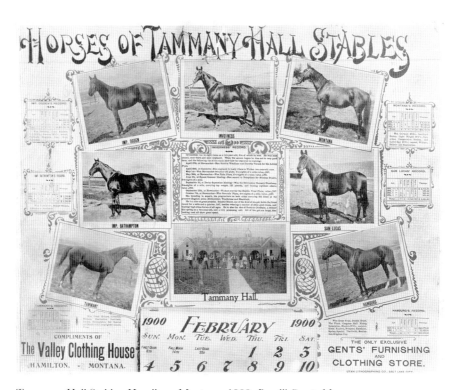

Tammany Hall Stables, Hamilton, Montana, 1900. *Ravalli County Museum.*

Daly's horse racing passion provides further evidence of the Tammany influence. Racehorse names often reflect aspects of their owner's life or interests, and Daly named his favorite racehorse Tammany. In turn, Tammany sired foals named Tammany Hall and Grand Sachem—the title given the leaders of Tammany Hall. In 1900, the Bitterroot Stock Farm's Thoroughbred Division was advertised as "Tammany Hall Stables."

Tammany Hall was not the only influence on the adolescent Daly. He also lived in New York at the same time as an émigré who appealed to an Irishman's noble impulses.

THE IRISH HERO

Born in Waterford, Ireland, well-educated and articulate, Thomas Francis Meagher (1823–1867) became a fiery nationalist who introduced the green, white, and orange Irish "tricolour" flag to the world on March 7, 1848.

His drive for Irish freedom led to an unfortunate outcome: for his role in that year's Young Ireland Uprising, the British exiled Meagher in lieu of hanging, sending him to Van Diemen's Land (now Tasmania, Australia). He escaped the island, and when he reached New York City in 1852, his arrival was announced with great fanfare. He became a noted orator and hero to the Irish diaspora.[91]

In 1856, Meagher launched the *Irish News*, a voice of Irish nationalism in America that soon had a circulation of fifty thousand. If Daly hawked newspapers, it is possible Meagher's was one he sold. As an adult, Daly was interested in news from and about Ireland and regularly read another nationalist paper, the *Irish World and American Industrial Liberator*.[92]

Thomas Francis Meagher, circa 1865. *National Archives.*

It is unlikely that a young Marcus Daly personally knew the famous revolutionary, but Daly may have witnessed Meagher's speeches. If Daly's father Luke was a member of the Young Ireland movement in County Cavan, Meagher may have been a household name.

Meagher later played a significant role in Montana history, serving as acting territorial governor from 1865 until his highly suspicious death in 1867. Although Daly did not reach Montana until well after Meagher's passing, Daly's leadership of the project to commemorate Meagher hints at passionate Irish patriotism.[93] While Daly's own monument did not immortalize him astride a fine horse, he put another Irishman on one.

RICH AND POOR, WORK AND PLAY

Greater New York ran on muscle in 1856. Ships and steam locomotives brought passengers and freight to the then-separate cities of New York and Brooklyn, but the "last mile" required humans to unload cargo, while horses and mules hauled goods, pulled fire wagons, and conveyed people in taxis, streetcars, and ambulances. Fine carriages promenaded through Central

Park, which opened in 1857, while mounted couriers dashed from place to place on nimble horses—much as bicyclists do today.[94]

There was manure everywhere, even in the most elegant neighborhoods. The gap between the rich and the poor played out in the animal kingdom as well as in human tenements. The career of a streetcar horse could be as short as two years and seldom more than five. Yet while horses sometimes died on the streets in their traces, on the turf, they were royalty.[95]

When Daly reached America, harness racing with trotting horses had become the nation's first mass-spectator sport. Ordinary people could race the same horse they used for daily travel. Like modern stock car racing, it was a populist contrast to class-conscious running races with "blooded" Thoroughbreds and wealthy owners who hired trainers and jockeys. As Frank Forester explained, harness racing was "the people's sport, the people's pastime, and consequently, is, and will be, supported by the people."[96]

The racetrack was a magnet to anyone seeking excitement, and by 1858, there were at least seven in the greater New York area. Daly could have watched races while on a break from cleaning stables, standing along the backside rail. Or perhaps, after unloading ship cargo, he took a ferry or streetcar to stake out a free spot with the masses in the track infield. He even could have spent precious pennies on admission to stand along the homestretch rail, where rich and poor seamlessly rubbed elbows. Daly lived Lord George Bentinck's adage: "All men are equal on and under the turf."[97]

Daly knew how to drive horses, and the trotting tracks of greater New York had an influence on him. Not only did Conrad Kohrs note his ability to drive a fast buggy, but Daly burst onto Montana's racing scene in 1886 with trotters.

Though harness racing was popular, its amateur practitioners were not. They were dismissed as fast men "who spent their afternoons trotting from tavern to tavern." Impromptu street races created traffic hazards. Organized contests were dogged with accusations that races were fixed and that the owners conspired in "hippodroming"—setting up races with no actual purse money paid to the winner, just an agreement that all contestants would split the gate receipts.[98]

When winter snows arrived, sleighing season reigned in the city streets, and racing lightweight one-horse "cutters" was immortalized in song.[99] Today, "Jingle Bells" is a Christmas carol, but when it was published in 1857, it was a popular hit, "One Horse Open Sleigh." It was a nineteenth-century

Top: The gap between rich and poor played out in the animal kingdom. "Broadway: Burst of Sunlight After a Shower," 1860. *NYPL.*

Bottom: "Close of a Career in New York," circa 1900. *LOC.*

Top: "Fast trotters on Harlem Lane," Currier and Ives, 1870. *NYPL.*

Bottom: Sleighing in New York, 1855. *NYPL.*

predecessor to twentieth-century songs such as "Born to Run" and other odes glorifying young men who chased speed, danger, and young women:

> *Now the ground is white*
> *Go it while you're young*
> *Take the girls tonight*
> *And sing this sleighing song*
> *Just get a bobtailed bay*
> *Two-forty as his speed*
> *Then hitch him to an open sleigh*
> *And crack! You'll take the lead!*
>
> *—from James Lord Pierpont, "Jingle Bells," or "The One-Horse Open Sleigh"*

Just as young people in modern car culture "cruise main" on a Saturday night, as a teenager, Daly probably wanted to be among the young men driving swift trotting horses to win money, drinks, or the attention of a pretty girl. The only question is whether he had opportunities to do so or if he merely shoveled manure and rubbed down tired livery horses late at night.

A DIVIDED NATION

In the New York of Daly's adolescence, good times at the races were, at best, a distraction from the problems facing mid-nineteenth century America. In 1857, a worldwide financial panic sent the economy into a tailspin, and the U.S. Supreme Court's *Dred Scott* decision upended the fragile balance between slave and free states. Tensions escalated until April 12, 1861, when the South Carolina militia opened fire on Fort Sumter in Charleston Harbor, launching the Civil War.

War presented nineteen-year-old Daly with difficult choices. Tammany Hall politicians, with commercial ties to the South and Copperhead sympathies, encouraged strong Irish laborers to stay and work in the city. Meanwhile, Thomas Francis Meagher was all in for the Union. His rousing speeches encouraged the Irish to don the blue. Meagher recruited and led the Fighting Sixty-Ninth, later the Irish Brigade, whose valor and blood showed the Know-Nothings—and everyone else—that Irish people belonged in America.[100]

It appears that Daly chose not to pick a side. While he could have kept a paying job on the docks or taken a military enlistment bonus, neither won the day. In 1861, he boarded a ship and headed to California.

LATE TO THE GOLD RUSH

Daly reached California in 1861, traveling by sea, supposedly on the "cheapest ticket obtainable." Family drew him west—his sister Anna and her husband, John O'Farrell, preceded him. They settled in Placer County, near Auburn. There is little detail known about Daly's time in California, but he described those years as "rough ones, and the hard knocks brought with them quite a bit of common sense." Molly Gerard told K. Ross Toole, "What he did there [in California], I don't know. He worked his way to Virginia City [Nevada] by doing all kinds of odd jobs."[101]

California reeled from massive changes. In less than one hundred years, the land passed from Native control to the Spanish, then to Mexico and ultimately the United States. Hunter-gatherers gave way to missionaries and *rancheros*, then miners. After gold was discovered, those who obtained vast new fortunes usually were not the original prospectors but those who bought them out, including George Hearst, James Ben Ali Haggin, and Lloyd Tevis, the triumvirate who became Daly's business partners in 1881.

Daly reached California over a decade after the initial gold rush, when wealth had moved from placer gold panning in streams to blasting and shoveling rock in underground lode mines. There, Daly first learned the trade that led to his fortune.

It is unclear how long Daly stayed in California. Various accounts have him heading for Nevada as early as 1862, but he was first documented there in 1865. With work on both sides of the Sierra Nevada Range, the restless young man may have moved frequently from place to place.[102]

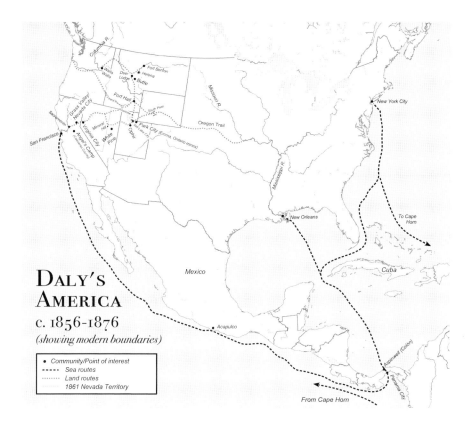

DALY'S
AMERICA
c. 1856-1876
(showing modern boundaries)

- Community/Point of interest
---- Sea routes
······ Land routes
—— 1861 Nevada Territory

OCEANS WEST

Over half of all travelers to Gold Rush–era California came by ship. The cheapest berths sailed around Cape Horn, a five- to eight-month-long journey. Daly did not actually select that "cheapest ticket"; he took the faster and more expensive route via the Isthmus of Panama. Daly might have worked for his fare; an 1862 advertisement promoted a steerage berth for $100 (about $2,700 in 2020 dollars). In ideal conditions, the trip took less than a month via steamship or about fifty days by sail. There were dangers beyond bad weather; with the Civil War on, Union-flagged vessels were vulnerable to Confederate raiders.[103]

Daly's experiences may have paralleled those of William Brewer, a young scientist with the first California Geological Survey. Brewer took a steamship from New York on October 22, 1860, reaching Aspinwall (now Colón) in eight days. Riding the Panama Railway across the isthmus took a day and

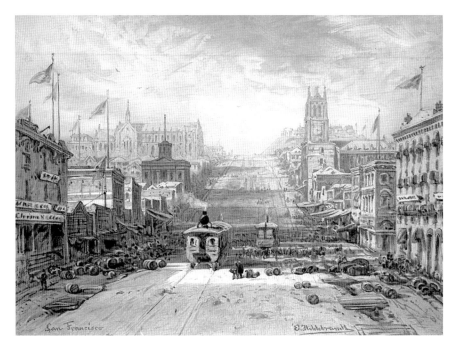

San Francisco, circa 1862. *Bancroft.*

cost twenty-five dollars. After a short layover, Brewer left Panama City on a mail steamer, where he shared a six-by-six-foot "stateroom" with three other people, so he usually spent the tropical nights sleeping on the open deck. On November 14, Brewer's ship reached the Golden Gate and anchored in San Francisco Bay.

Brewer viewed lush jungle vegetation in Panama, snacked on new, exotic fruits such as bananas, marveled at grand views of volcanic peaks, and griped about the humidity. A swift Panama City layover like Brewer's was not guaranteed; many travelers faced delays of days or even weeks awaiting the arrival of northbound ships. If Daly had to wait, he could have indulged his favorite vice: spending idle days betting on local horse races.[104]

San Francisco was still raw and boisterous when Daly arrived, but it was the largest city west of the Mississippi, fast approaching a population of sixty thousand. Its wide streets with buildings of brick and granite gave it the look of a well-established metropolis. Its climate, milder than New York or Ballyjamesduff, allowed colorful flowers to bloom everywhere.[105]

People from all over the world flocked to the City by the Bay. Dozens of languages filled Daly's ears, including a familiar accent—the Irish made up roughly 9 percent of California's population. On the bustling streets and wharfs, he rubbed elbows with Asians, Mexicans, and free Black people—all of whom struggled for basic human rights. Women—at least white women—were a distinct minority; according to the 1860 federal census, only about 30 percent of Californians were female.[106] At the bottom of the social scale were California's decimated Native people.

EDEN TRANSFORMED

Daly arrived in a land transformed by colonialism as surely as British conquest and the Great Famine transformed Ireland. The estimated pre-Columbian population of California was over three hundred thousand—the most densely populated region of what today is the United States. In 1769, a permanent Spanish population arrived. Native people were forcibly converted to Christianity, pressed into land-bound peonage, died of disease, or fled.

When Mexico won independence from Spain in 1821, the Mexican government expanded Spain's land grant system, establishing *ranchos*, which covered nearly fourteen thousand square miles of California's richest agricultural land. Owners were essentially feudal lords over thousands of acres. The cattle industry dominated the economy, and livestock were managed by *vaqueros*, horsemen mostly of mixed-race *Mestizo* ancestry trained in centuries-old Spanish traditions.[107]

When the Mexican War broke out in 1846, American settlers organized the Bear Flag Revolt and declared California a republic. The conflict ended with the 1848 Treaty of Guadalupe Hidalgo, which transferred significant territory to the United States. Soon after, gold discoveries at Sutter's Mill triggered a massive influx of fortune-seekers from around the world, the "forty-niners" of the California Gold Rush. In 1850, California became a state.

Officially a free state, the disingenuously named Act for the Government and Protection of Indians authorized forced labor of Native people, creating de facto slavery and widespread violence from farm fields to mining camps. By 1870, Native people were one-tenth their pre-Columbian population.[108]

For the vaqueros, both miners and rancheros needed beef, so they kept their horses and their jobs. The new boss was not so different from the old boss. A navy chaplain, Walter Colton, the first American *Alcalde* of Monterey, was a candid observer. He noted:

The Californian is most at home in his saddle.…His horse, with his long flowing mane, arching neck, broad chest, full flanks, and slender legs, is full of fire.…On his back is the Californian's home. Leave him this home, and you may have the rest of the world.[109]

Though the Gold Rush took over the rest of the *Californianos'* world, uniquely *Mexicano* forms of song and dance remained, incorporating Spanish, African, and Native elements. When Colton further commented, "The dance and a dashing horse are the two objects which overpower all others in interest with the Californians," he could have described a youthful Marcus Daly, the "fun-loving fellow" who arrived a decade later.[110]

Another battleground was found in the courts. *Rancho* owners who held land grants clashed with new arrivals from the eastern United States. The losers were those who could not produce documentation of their grants—or who failed to defend their legal ownership. The winners included George Hearst, James Ben Ali Haggin, and Lloyd Tevis.[111]

HEARST, HAGGIN, AND TEVIS

The three men who revolutionized Daly's life reached California long before he did.

George Hearst (1820–1891) grew up in Franklin County, Missouri. He reached California in 1850 and speculated in the quartz gold region around Grass Valley and Nevada City. Hearst swore freely, chewed tobacco, and lived a bathing-optional lifestyle. But he made friends easily, later entered California politics, and ultimately became a United States senator.[112]

In 1859, Hearst realized that blue-black ore samples coming from the Washoe District on the east side of the Sierra Nevada Range contained silver. They came from a mine promoted by a grifter named Henry Comstock, who allegedly obtained his shares for $40.00, a bottle of whiskey, and a half-blind horse. Hearst grabbed a one-sixth share of Comstock's mine and snapped up several other claims. He organized the Ophir Silver Mining Company and took out forty-five tons of silver ore within the year, worth $5.04 million at the time. It established his fortune.[113]

The Washoe, then part of Utah Territory, split off, becoming Nevada Territory in 1861. Its vast silver deposits became known as the Comstock lode. Hearst returned to Missouri and, in 1862, wed a schoolteacher named

Left: George Hearst, 1887. *LOC.*

Right: Phoebe Apperson Hearst holding an infant William Randolph Hearst, circa 1863. *Bancroft.*

Phoebe Apperson (1842–1919). He sweetened the deal with a prenuptial agreement, giving her 4,800 shares in the Gould and Curry Gold and Silver Mining Company, worth about $2.4 million. In 1863, she gave birth to their only child, William Randolph Hearst.[114]

George saw Phoebe settled in the best luxury San Francisco could offer and then returned to the mining camps. They lived in separate spheres, though she cleaned him up enough that, in 1865, he was elected to the California State Assembly, launching his political career.[115]

Lloyd Tevis (1824–1899) and James Ben Ali Haggin (1822–1914) were Kentuckians, sons of lawyers who grew up within an echelon of small slaveholder families. Tevis studied law, but drawn to finance, he became a salesman and then a banker. He left for California around 1849. An indifferent prospector, Tevis soon found a desk job at the county recorder's office in Sacramento, where tracking land deeds alerted him to investment opportunities.[116]

Haggin's maternal grandfather was a Turkish physician, Ibrahim Ben Ali. Said to resemble his grandfather, Haggin was proud of his heritage. He gave the name Ben Ali as the middle name for two of his children and to his racehorse that won the 1886 Kentucky Derby. It is uncertain how much racism played a role in his life, but Haggin had little career success

Left: Lloyd Tevis. *Wikimedia Commons.*

Right: James Ben Ali Haggin, circa 1870. *Haggin Museum, Stockton, California.*

in Kentucky. He had better luck practicing law in multiethnic Natchez, Mississippi. There, he met another former Kentuckian, Eliza Jane Sanders (1823–1894), whom he married in 1846. Soon after, he expanded his law practice to New Orleans.[117]

Haggin left for California in 1850. He booked a speedy steamship passage from New Orleans to Aspinwall, but hit miserable conditions in Panama. There was no railroad across the isthmus until 1855, so he traveled upriver by rowboat to Culebra Summit, then on foot with his belongings on pack mules to Panama City. Waiting a month for a ship, he witnessed riots and survived yellow fever. Haggin later described with delight his first glimpse of San Francisco Bay, arriving "on a glorious Sunday morning."[118]

In California, Haggin reconnected with Tevis. They opened a law and land office in Sacramento, handling real estate deals and loaning money at high interest rates. In 1853, they moved their operation to San Francisco. Eliza and the Haggin children arrived soon after, along with her sister Susan, who married Tevis in 1854.[119]

The brothers-in-law invested widely: land, livestock, telegraphs, stagecoach lines, railroads, steamships, banks, and mining properties. Their personalities meshed. Tevis was an outgoing salesman and aggressive negotiator who boasted he could "think five times as fast than any man in San Francisco." But underneath, he was cautious and risk adverse. Haggin, quiet and cool-headed, was the gambler. He would masterfully bide his time, then take bold risks that usually paid off.[120]

The nineteenth-century press labeled Haggin "a sultan" or "the Turk" for his ethnicity and shrewd business dealings. It was worse behind closed doors. One example occurred in 1889, when Daly's archnemesis W.A. Clark poured fat on the fiery Clark-Daly feud by describing Haggin—who supported Daly—with a coarse racial slur.[121]

It is unclear when Haggin and Tevis met Hearst, but by 1860, they invested together. They needed one another: Haggin and Tevis owned mining properties but had little mining knowledge, and Hearst had the "nose for ore" but needed outside capital plus the expertise of bankers and lawyers. Forming Hearst, Haggin, Tevis, and Company, the trio dominated American mining until Hearst's death in 1891.[122]

There is little study of their personal interactions, but all three men had a need for speed. Haggin and Hearst were drawn to the racetrack. Hearst knew the value of social lubrication in business and spent $200,000 to build San Francisco's Bay View Park Racetrack in 1863. The long gaps between races were, ostensibly, time for spectators to assess horses and place wagers. But the wealthy discussed business and politics at the clubhouse or in their private grandstand boxes.[123]

For Haggin, born in Bluegrass country, his love of horses went beyond recreation or status. It was "bred in the bone." He drove a magnificent carriage through San Francisco's city parks on Sundays, pulled by four matching coach horses in silver-trimmed harness. It was the nineteenth-century version of a Rolls-Royce. His California horse operation, the forty-four-thousand-acre Rancho del Paso, became the largest horse-breeding establishment in the world, and in many ways inspired Daly's Bitter Root Stock Farm in Montana.[124]

In contrast to Hearst and Haggin, Tevis was abstemious, "little disposed to the sports of the turf and field." Yet Tevis ran express mail couriers on swift horses throughout California and Nevada well after the end of the Pony Express. They inspired his grandson Will Tevis, who supported Wendell Robie's 1955 efforts to organize the famed Western States Trail Ride, a one-hundred-mile horse endurance race from Tahoe City to Auburn. It is popularly known today as the Tevis Cup, after the championship trophy named in memory of Lloyd Tevis.[125]

Auburn, California, circa 1861. The Orleans Hotel is the building with a balcony near the center. *Inset*: Sacajawea with an infant Jean-Baptiste Charbonneau, also known as "Pomp." *LOC, U.S. Mint.*

AUBURN

It is no surprise an endurance contest ends in Auburn. It was an early gold rush town near the end of the California Trail, where travelers could stop for supplies, a night's rest, a hot meal, and a few drinks. The area was home to Anna and John O'Farrell for about a decade, and there, Anna gave birth to at least four of her six children.[126]

A figure from early Montana history lived in Auburn at the same time as the O'Farrells: Jean-Baptiste "J.B." Charbonneau (1805–1866). Best known to history as "Pompey" or "Pomp," he was the youngest member of the 1804–6 Lewis and Clark Expedition—the baby Sacajawea carried on her back as the Corps of Discovery traveled through Montana to the Pacific Ocean and back. Later, William Clark (not to be confused with Daly's nemesis, William Andrews Clark) paid for his education.

Becoming a frontier guide, Charbonneau scouted the first wagon route to southern California in 1846 and then remained in the far west. Between 1860 and 1866, Charbonneau ran the Orleans Hotel in Auburn. There, he was known as "intelligent, well-read in the topics of the day, and…generally esteemed." Charbonneau left Auburn for Montana in 1866 but took ill along the way and died before reaching his destination.[127]

As with Meagher in New York, it is unknown if Daly met Charbonneau. But it is a near certainty that Daly visited his sister. What else he did in Auburn is conjecture, but it would be no surprise if Daly drank at the Orleans. News of Charbonneau's departure or death could be how Daly first heard of a place called Montana.

FARMS AND FLOODS

Some stories claim Daly struggled to find a job in California, but finding work was not difficult—an 1856 advertisement offered unskilled laborers double the wages available in New York City. The problem was that wages fluctuated wildly. Daly was one of thousands of anxious, ambitious young men, collectively described as "a combination of mutability and recklessness." Miners earned between three and twelve dollars a day, and in 1861, wages were on the low end, while living expenses remained at inflated gold rush levels.[128]

Daly may have sold newspapers in San Francisco, but if he did, it was not for long. An 1893 newspaper told a tale that Daly's first job was digging potatoes, which is possible. Many "truck farms" supplied food to the city. William Scallon recalled Daly saying he had done some "farming."[129]

Raised in rural County Cavan, Daly was familiar with agricultural work, and it was easily found. Cattle and crops produced wealth described as a "second gold rush." But this bubble also burst. Daly reached California just before a natural disaster—courtesy of a phenomenon now called an "atmospheric river."

It started raining in November 1861 and rarely let up until February 1862. The entire state was inundated. The gold rush town of Sonora reported sixty-nine days of rain, totaling seventy-two inches. The Sierras saw over ten feet of early snow, which melted during a freak warm spell in December.[130]

Precipitation and snowmelt, flowing into riverbeds clogged by a decade of placer mining sediment, led to disaster. In January 1862, William Brewer wrote, "Thousands of farms are entirely underwater." Stockton newspapers declared, "As far as the eye can see, a vast inland sea spreads." Roads were washed out. Food was scarce. San Francisco charities sent

"Inundation of the State Capitol," flooding in Sacramento, 1862. *California State Library.*

steamers of relief supplies upriver to the devastated city of Sacramento, where the river rose twenty-two feet, topped telegraph poles, and forced the legislature from the capitol.[131]

Flooding destroyed one-fourth of the taxable property in the state. Mining camps saw ruined equipment, drowned shafts, and washed-out diggings. Hundreds of thousands of animal carcasses choked the land. The deluge of sediment-contaminated freshwater flowing to the sea destroyed the oyster beds at Oakland. The human toll was significant: the Chinese community tracked their statewide losses and reported 1,400 casualties.[132]

Disaster also presented opportunities. A great deal of land changed hands in the aftermath. In 1862, Haggin and Tevis foreclosed on a $64,000 note owed to them by Samuel Norris, obtaining Rancho del Paso. Norris claimed he was cheated and litigated the issue until 1890, when the U.S. Supreme Court settled the matter in favor of Haggin. Floodwaters also scoured mine tailings from riverbeds, exposing fresh rock and new sources of gold. This caused a temporary revival of independent prospecting, which correlates with sources that state Daly headed for the diggings in 1862.[133]

Daly Becomes a Miner

California's early prospectors found gold by placer mining—scooping rock out of streambeds, using water to separate out nuggets and gold dust. The iconic solo forty-niner with his burro, pickaxe, and gold pan quickly teamed up with others. To make serious money, miners sent gravel and flowing water through sluice boxes, rockers, and other trough-like devices with riffle bars to separate gold from waste rock. After miners scoured the streambeds, they brought in equipment for hydraulic mining, shooting water from high pressure hoses to dislodge gold-laden alluvium from streambanks. Soon, most surface gold was gone.[134]

Riches were still buried deep in the mountains. Lode mining required blasting and digging into hard rock quartz formations, revealing gold at its source. The need for capital segregated miners into owners, managers, and

Placer mining, 1866. *LOC.*

Hydraulic mining, Montana territory, circa 1880. California miners used similar technology in the 1860s. *BSB.*

laborers. Prospectors reassessed their careers. Some, like Henry Comstock, sought placer gold elsewhere. Others, like Lloyd Tevis, took up different professions. Marcus Daly joined the wage laborers, working for those with funds for equipment, employees, and ever-deeper holes in the ground.[135]

Daly met a fellow Irishman, Thomas Murray (circa 1827–1903), who mentored Daly's fledgling mining career, giving the young man a horse and a grubstake. Two decades later, Daly returned the favor, making Murray a watchman and then a yard foreman at the Anaconda smelter. In California, the pair built a cabin somewhere near Placerville, where they spent a winter and tried prospecting. It apparently was not going particularly well when Murray caught word of job opportunities in Calaveras County.[136]

Calaveras was a mountainous land dotted with rough mining towns like Angel's Camp. According to Hugh Daly's account, when Daly and Murray joined a line of jobseekers, a local bully went after them, saying, "There are already too many greenhorn Irish in this camp." In response, Daly punched the fellow on the chin and knocked him out. This act allegedly impressed the foreman, who hired Daly and Murray on the spot.[137]

There were plenty of "Irish" around—and not just greenhorns. Some ran the mines. One owner in Angel's Camp was James Fair from County

Tyrone, and he later became one of the "Bonanza Kings" of Nevada's Comstock lode. Daly knew Fair in Nevada; it is possible their paths crossed in Calaveras.[138]

Daly most likely started as a "mucker," an unskilled worker who shoveled rock into ore carts. In 1899, a newspaper story claimed his first job was at the What Cheer mine. Like other tales about Daly, a highly specific local detail could be accurate, even in an otherwise error-riddled account. The same story had another unique angle, claiming Daly and other young miners sought recreation in the town of Jackson, about thirty miles to the northwest. There, according to the story, "several young ladies made life pleasant," and years later, after Daly made his fortune, he supposedly sent them some fine pianos.[139]

Calaveras County also hosted a mine at Copperopolis, about fifteen miles southwest of Angel's Camp. In the 1860s, Copperopolis was the second-highest producer of copper ore in the United States, only surpassed by the famed mines of Michigan's Upper Peninsula. Copper was a critical strategic resource for the Union during the Civil War, used in munitions, telegraphs, and alloys such as brass and bronze.[140]

In 1865, Charles T. Meader, described by historian Harry Freeman as "the true father of copper mining in the whole West," completed a blast furnace at Copperopolis and smelted the first copper in California. In 1876, Meader came to Butte City, Montana Territory—the same year Daly arrived.[141]

Daly left Calaveras in 1862 or 1863 and headed for Nevada County, California. He worked in gold mines near Grass Valley and Nevada City. According to biographer Minar Shoebotham, this is where Daly traded his mucker's shovel for the single jack and double jack—chisels struck with sledgehammers to hand-drill holes into rock. Daly most likely became familiar with every step of mining, from blast to bullion. Lode mining began with the dangerous art of packing holes with black powder (or after 1867, dynamite) and setting off explosions. Ore was sorted from gangue, or waste rock, then fed into mills built near the mines, where piston-driven stamps crushed or "reduced" the ore into fine particles. Adding mercury and heat to crushed ore amalgamated and extracted the gold.[142]

Daly liked Nevada County enough that in 1880, he declared he would retire to Grass Valley. As explained in chapter 7, it was a plausible-sounding ruse Daly used to deceive his competition about his multiple trips to California, seeking funding from Hearst, Haggin, and Tevis for his Anaconda mine in Butte, Montana.[143]

Work and Play

When work was over and wages were collected, no one played harder than miners. Bored, lonely men with loose gold dust "bet on anything and everything"—foot races and horse races, drilling competitions, and even saloon wagers on which table a fly might land. Blood sports such as cockfights and dogfights were routine. A grizzly bear named General Scott drew $4,000 in stakes to battle a Spanish bull. Though ever-tougher morality legislation was passed every time the state legislature met in Sacramento, Sunday—the miners' day off—remained race day.[144]

In mining country, match races ran down dirt streets, and small "bullring" ovals occupied patches of flat ground. Grass Valley and Calaveras County each had at least two marked courses.[145] If he had a horse, Daly may have participated in informal races. Given his known fondness for betting, he surely placed wagers.

While fast horses and the thrill of a bet lightened Daly's Sundays, actual horsepower shaped everyday life. Animals were living machines. Pack strings and harnessed freight teams hauled ore out of the mountains. Until steam power arrived, horses and mules spent endless days walking in a circle; they powered the arastra, dragging flat-bottomed three-hundred- to five-hundred-pound boulders to pulverize ore against a paved stone surface. Hitched to a rotary arm on a crankshaft, they also powered the whim, a hoist used to raise and lower workers, supplies, and ore.[146]

Later, the Daly legend told tales of Montana's wealthy and powerful Copper King exhibiting compassion not only for his elite racehorses but also for working animals. One story comes from the town of Anaconda, founded by Daly in 1883 with the assistance of his friend and agent Morgan Evans. According to Shoebotham, the two men and Evans's son Billy were driving a carriage through town when Billy asked them to stop. Jumping from the carriage, the boy ran over to a limping workhorse, picked up the horse's hoof, pulled out a pocketknife, and dislodged a stone. Then Daly stepped down from the carriage and ordered the driver to unhitch the horse from the wagon. Taking the bridle, Daly handed the reins to Billy and said that the horse now belonged to the boy, leaving the driver and his load stranded in the street.[147]

This anecdote could be a morality tale akin to the story of George Washington chopping down the cherry tree—Shoebotham's account contains fictional embellishments. As a description of Daly's character, it shows his willingness to dress down an employee as an example to everyone

Arastra, 1850. *From* Frost's Pictorial History of California.

Hoist and horse whim, Butte, Montana (undated). *BSB.*

on the payroll. On the other hand, it suggests Daly knew the toll of working life on both man and beast.

Few extant photographs clearly show Daly's hands, but in one, a gnarled, mangled pointer finger provides physical evidence of his hard knocks. As he finished his California mining apprenticeship, Daly's next steps took him across the Sierra Nevada Range to better fortune.

PART II

THE SILVER YEARS

ON THE COMSTOCK

In mining country, tales abounded of the "Big One," a gold strike always over the next hill. For post–gold rush California, the Big One was over the Sierra Nevada Range—and contained silver. The mines of the Washoe region produced over $300 million in their time, equivalent to billions of dollars today. The boomtown of Virginia City, Nevada, grew in the shadow of Mount Davidson, eventually boasting a population of twenty-five thousand people. Carson City, the capital of the territory, opened a branch of the U.S. Mint in 1863.[148]

Nevada became a state in 1864, but its silver boom slumped soon after. Work remained for the strong and reliable, but steady work was not guaranteed. Miners frequently moved, working both sides of the California-Nevada line. Many miners traveled on foot, "carrying their blankets" from camp to camp. Some hitched rides on freight wagons or hired on to escort a pack train. A decent mount could be had for about thirty dollars, affordable at wages of twelve dollars a day but a challenge at the typical four dollars a day paid on the Comstock.[149]

Once it was obvious that the Comstock lode held silver, many gold miners left for Colorado, Idaho, and Montana. Henry Comstock sold out for $11,000 and then drifted from camp to camp, dying by suicide in 1870 near Bozeman, Montana. Meanwhile, the capitalists reaped millions. Lloyd Tevis focused on transportation, express mail, and banking. Haggin and Hearst consolidated the partnership's mining investments.[150]

Virginia City, Nevada, 1867. *LOC.*

Freight wagons and pack mules carried a steady flow of silver over the mountains to California. Primitive trails became two-way roads—complete with traffic jams involving everything from stagecoaches to twenty-mule wagon teams. Wells Fargo and other express mail companies sent relay riders from Carson City to San Francisco in as little as two days. In good weather, stagecoaches from Nevada's Gold Hill reached Sacramento in twenty-four hours. From Sacramento, steamboats and railroads transported goods and people to the coast.[151]

According to lawyer and journalist C.P. Connolly, Daly reached Nevada in 1863. Most likely, he drifted back and forth across the Sierra Nevada Range at first, but once settled, he stayed in Nevada for about five years. He jumped into the social life of the Irish community. True to his Irish roots, in November 1865, "Mark Daley" served on the invitations committee for the Fenian Brotherhood's Grand Ball in Silver City, marking the first time his name appeared in print.[152]

Daly reached the Silver State as technology revolutionized the west with steam power and ever-more complex mining equipment. Railroads began creeping up steep grades and over the Sierras. The Virginia & Truckee

Teamsters in winter descending from the summit of the Sierra Nevada Range, 1866. *LOC.*

Railroad reached Virginia City in 1869, the same year Leland Stanford tapped in a golden spike at Promontory Summit, Utah Territory, completing the transcontinental railroad.[153]

DALY AND HEARST

Daly probably knew of George Hearst well before they met. The relationship between the two men was complex. Various accounts claim Daly worked in Hearst's mines prior to their Anaconda partnership, which is possible, but solid documentation has yet to be located. The first evidence of a business connection is their 1872 meeting in Utah. Most accounts vaguely state they became acquainted in "Nevada"—either the state or the California county is possible, as Hearst had business interests throughout the region. Daly legends portray the two as friends, but the weight of the evidence suggests cooler, businesslike interactions.

A popular but dubious tale claims they met in 1864. The year could be right, but the story, like others surrounding Daly, is an error-riddled mashup of unrelated events with fictional embellishments.

The story claims that Phoebe Hearst worried about her husband's lengthy absence during a trip to British Columbia, so she asked Daly to lead a search party to find him. Allegedly, his search took him through Montana's Bitterroot Valley and was his first view of Montana.[154]

The accurate part is that Hearst did scout and reject a claim near Lake Kootenay in British Columbia sometime between 1864 and 1868. But independent accounts do not indicate Hearst was deemed missing, nor do they mention Daly. Further, Phoebe Hearst disliked George's long absences, but they were common; the Hearsts lived separate lives. Had she hired a search party, which was unlikely, Phoebe's support came from her own family and connections. She distrusted George's associates, including Tevis and Haggin. Later, when selling her Anaconda Company shares in 1896, she also vented to a friend about Daly's underhanded dealings.[155]

Geographic logic rules out a Montana route. Hearst traveled to Canada via the Columbia River, starting from Colville, Washington Territory. The Bitterroot Valley was hundreds of miles farther east, an illogical detour.

That said, according to a 1937 account, Hearst did get lost in the Bitterroot Valley when Daly and Hearst went there in the 1880s, scouting timber for the Anaconda mine. That story claimed the late summer meadows were so lush that grass grew taller than the head of a man on a horse, and disoriented, Hearst "had to stay out all night."[156]

The most probable account of Daly's first view of the Bitterroot comes from an 1898 story in the *American Turf*. It mentioned that Daly saw the area when he was "at the head of a relief party." That account claimed the event occurred "in the sixties" but does not mention Hearst. Notwithstanding the date, the "relief party" most likely referred to the time Daly helped evacuate wounded soldiers after the 1877 Battle of the Big Hole.[157]

Daly and Mackay

One of the biggest winners in Nevada was Daly's mentor, John W. Mackay (1831–1902). A solid role model, Mackay was well-liked, even though he was exacting, short-tempered, and had a stutter. He worked alongside his men, was willing to do any job he asked of another, and paid close attention to worker safety.[158]

John Mackay, circa 1890. *Bancroft.*

Mackay was born poor in Ireland, where his family shared a dirt-floored hovel with the family pig. Like Daly, he spent some of his youth hawking papers in New York City, then in his twentieth year came west. Mackay reached California in 1851. Penniless when he walked into the Washoe mining camps in 1859, Mackay's fortunes soon improved. By 1863, he was a manager and owned shares in various mines. His big break came in 1865 with his partnership in the "Kentuck," where a rich vein of mixed silver and gold launched his fortune.[159]

It is not known where or when Mackay first employed Daly. Possibilities include the Milton, where Mackay was a superintendent in 1863. Another possibility is that Daly worked in the Kentuck. But Mackay spotted Daly's ability to lead others and made him a shift boss. Daly's career path mirrored Mackay's. Both started at the bottom, managed mines where they earned the respect of their workers, and finally established their fortunes with solid partnerships. Daly's leadership style more closely resembled that of Mackay than of anyone else, but this is not surprising—both Irishmen understood the role of the *ceann fine*. Daly was like Mackay: "loyal to men above him and devoted to those beneath."[160]

Molly Gerard stated that the two men were lifelong friends. In 1900, Mackay, then one of the richest men in America, was a pallbearer at Daly's funeral. Daly's remains were interred in the Mackay family mausoleum at Brooklyn's Green-Wood Cemetery until his own family crypt was completed.[161]

Daly worked for people aside from Mackay. According to Connolly, Daly's first Nevada boss was Bill Skyrme (circa 1835–1925). Nicknamed "Scarrum," Wales-born Skyrme reached the Comstock in 1860, becoming

Marcus Daly (*standing*), with Bill Skyrme. A 1906 lithograph from a photograph taken circa 1863 in San Francisco. The top hat worn by Daly was the first he ever owned. *Connolly, 454.*

foreman of the Savage mine and later the Hale & Norcross. Years later in Butte, Daly hired the aging Skyrme as a supervisor. Not caring that the tables had turned, Skyrme once ordered Daly to put out a cigar right in front of a group of wealthy investors touring the High Ore Mine.[162]

By 1873, Daly had left the Comstock. But that year, Mackay, James Fair, and the bartenders turned stock traders James Flood and William O'Brien became the "Bonanza Kings" when their Con Virginia mine hit the largest silver ore body ever found in North America.[163]

SPECULATORS AND TECHNOLOGY

Mining's boom-bust cycles had multiple triggers, ranging from vagaries of mineral veins to the whims of the market. Informal partnerships meant claimants wrangled over ownership. Legal fights tangled up some Comstock operations for years. Frequent sales with poor documentation meant the Washoe saw nearly as much "courthouse mining" as the real thing. Everyone scrambled for a piece of the action.

Members of the San Francisco Stock Exchange created havoc for short-term gain. Spectators notoriously manipulated the stock in an unregulated climate, fleecing unwary victims, and bankers were not above calling in miners' loans just as a new ore body was discovered, freezing out the working owner.[164]

The actual work of mining silver required both upfront capital and technical expertise. Sinking mine shafts thousands of feet underground pushed the development of new technologies. Comstock mines began using dynamite in 1868, increasing the power of explosive charges. Shafts and tunnels were shored up with massive square-set timbering to support the works. Large quantities of rock were hauled out, and the ore was separated from gangue and run through heavy stamp mills that pounded it into small particles. Then came the chemistry: reduced ore was dumped into giant iron pans, heated up and mixed with water, salt, copper sulfate, and mercury. Nevada's new type of large-scale pan amalgamation was called the "Washoe process," and it revolutionized silver mining.[165]

Humans sweated underground, drilling holes, setting explosives, shoveling ore, and hand-tramming ore carts—mules were not lowered into the Comstock mines until 1871. Accidents were rampant and deaths common; men fell down shafts, hoists failed, tunnels caved, pumps gave out, mines flooded, and ventilation was primitive. Fire was a constant threat.

"A Question of Title." *From J. Ross Browne, "A Peep at Washoe,"* Harper's Monthly, *January 1861.*

Comstock's miners earned their nickname: the "hot water boys." The deeper a shaft went, the hotter it got, and a layer of clay often concealed underground water, which was sometimes near boiling. In deep mine shafts, temperatures topped 120 degrees Fahrenheit. Ice was harvested from mountain lakes and reservoirs and then hauled into the mines. It saved lives; fans blew across the ice to cool the air, and it did double duty as it melted—miners drank up to four gallons of water per shift.[166]

Square set timbering and underground structures, Comstock mine, 1877. *Wikimedia Commons.*

Steam power came into its own, driving pumps that moved water and fans that circulated air. Stamp mills replaced arastras. Horse whims were succeeded by headframes to hoist people, ore, and equipment.

Mining's environmental consequences were enormous: entire forests were cut for timber and fuel, leaving denuded, eroded land. Water pumped from the mines discharged untreated contaminants. Waste from the Washoe process flushed into tailings piles. The air was filled with smoke from wood and coal, joined with dust from the surrounding land.[167]

The cultural consequences were equally as severe. The Washoe region was named for the Washoe people of the Lake Tahoe area who inhabited the region for centuries, but they lost access to their lands and water. The 1860 Pyramid Lake War, set off by atrocities committed by white men against two young Native girls, devastated the Paiute, Bannock, and Shoshone in the region.[168]

Daly and most other residents of Virginia City took each day as it came. Nevada's moralists tried valiantly to legislate behavior, but organized sin had a particularly strong foothold in Nevada. Theodore Winters (1823–1906), who invested with Hearst in the Ophir mine, summed up local sentiment. Around 1863, while serving in the territorial legislature, Winters declared, "It is more annoyance to me to hear a man praying too loud than to hear him hollering when he is drunk."[169] To the locals, Native culture and pristine forests were the past; the smells and sounds of mining were their present. The consequences were punted down the field to future generations.

The Holdup

Daly's Nevada sojourn overlapped that of Samuel L. Clemens, better known by his pen name, Mark Twain (1835–1910). Twain came west in 1861 and described his journey to Nevada in *Roughing It*, a "record of several years of variegated vagabondizing." Nevada's residents worked hard and played hard, and the story begins during the "wildest, most irresponsible and dangerous period of [Twain's] life."[170]

Twain took the quickest transport west: an overland stagecoach. Stage lines joined the nation, carrying mail, express freight, and passengers. Fares in 1860 were about $200 (roughly $4,500 in 2020), plus a dollar for every meal. Six to nine passengers crammed into any space—inside or out—that was not filled with freight. Drivers sat on top of the coach in all weather. Passengers were advised to bring their own firearms and were allowed twenty-five pounds of luggage. The conductor in charge of the trip literally "rode shotgun" by carrying a firearm while sitting next to the driver or riding a horse alongside—stages were frequent targets for theft.

Coaches were pulled by four to six horses or mules, swapped out at relay stations every ten to twenty miles, depending on the terrain. Stops were short, stages traveled at night, and passengers often slept on board the best they could. The speed record from St. Louis to Los Angeles was seventeen days, set in 1859. Twain claimed a trip from St. Joseph, Missouri, to Sacramento, California, could be done in fifteen. Mail contracts allowed twenty-five days of travel between St. Louis and San Francisco.[171]

Twain became a writer for the Virginia City *Territorial Enterprise*, where he first used his pen name. If Daly worked for Mackay or Skyrme in 1863, then he was in Nevada when Twain was on everyone's radar. The young newswriter freely mixed fact with fiction, flavoring his stories with biting

Stagecoach at Wells Fargo and Company's Express Office, Virginia City, Nevada, 1866. *LOC.*

satire. Locals declared him "the reigning loudmouth of Washoe." By 1864, Twain's over-the-top lampoons led to him receiving death threats, and he left Nevada for San Francisco.[172]

Twain's poison pen soon got him into trouble with newspapers in the Bay Area as well, so in the winter of 1864–65, he headed to Calaveras County. He laid low, staying at Jackass Hill near Angel's Camp with his friends Jim and Bill Gillis. There, he picked up any number of colorful tales. Inspired, he turned from journalism to fiction and immortalized the mining camps with his first successful short story, "The Celebrated Jumping Frog of Calaveras County."[173]

Twain's star rose, and he returned to Nevada in 1866 on his first speaking tour. Having previously offended more than a few people, he was anxious, but his lecture in Gold Hill on the night of November 10 was well received. Still, someone apparently felt he needed to be taken down a peg. Following his talk, Twain was the butt of an over-the-top practical joke—and Daly may have been involved.[174]

When Twain traveled back to Virginia City, six masked men accosted him and his agent. The leader held a loaded pistol to Twain's head while his accomplices emptied Twain's pockets of everything from his pencils to his treasured gold watch. The next day, the incident was revealed to be a prank. The ringleader was Twain's supposed friend Steve Gillis, who returned Twain's money and goods. Twain claimed he wasn't particularly frightened—though others begged to differ—but he was angry and left for San Francisco on the next stage.[175]

Daly was supposedly one of the six "robbers." Though evidence of Daly's

Mark Twain, age thirty-one, 1867. *LOC.*

involvement is scant, it is one of the more plausible situations where Daly was in the right place at the right time. Further, the prank fits other evidence that Daly was a "fun-loving fellow."[176]

Though Twain made no mention of Daly in his autobiography, their paths continued to intersect. On Twain's 1895 literary tour, he spoke in Butte and Anaconda and then stayed at Daly's Hotel Montana on August 2, a day when Daly was in Anaconda. Twain's loathing of Daly's chief rival, W.A. Clark, is well-documented, and notably, both Daly and Twain knew Henry Rogers of Standard Oil. Rogers was the vice-president of the Amalgamated Copper Company in 1899 and a pallbearer at Daly's funeral in 1900. For Twain, Rogers was a friend who helped him out of serious financial trouble.[177]

SHIFTING BORDERS

As rail lines crawled east from California to Utah, spurs headed to Nevada's mining camps, making it economically feasible to mine lower-grade ore in more remote areas. In addition, improvements in smelting technology made it possible to reduce the complex silver-lead ores discovered in Central Nevada between 1867 and 1869.[178]

Hearst's financial slump ended thanks to claims he purchased at Pioche and Mineral Hill. As new mines opened, politicians shifted Nevada's state border east to encompass them, eating away more of Utah Territory by moving the line from the 116th to the 115th meridian, and then settling it for good at the 114th.[179]

Meanwhile, Lloyd Tevis was thinking five times faster than anyone else. Realizing the transcontinental railroad would revolutionize banking and mail, he formed the Pacific Union Express, snagging an exclusive contract for express mail services with the Central Pacific and Union Pacific Railroads. He forced Wells Fargo and Company to merge with Pacific Union. By 1872, Tevis was president of Wells Fargo and Haggin was vice-president.[180]

Daly, as restless as Nevada's shifting eastern boundary, left the Comstock for the silver rush in Central Nevada, winding up at "Treasure Hill" in the White Pine area. Fortune-seekers poured in at the rate of over one hundred people per day. The boomtown population of Hamilton, Nevada, grew to twenty-four thousand people. In January 1869, the *Territorial Enterprise* interviewed Daly about the region, where he had been for two months, and his own words appeared for the first time in print. With a touch of Twain in his style, he declared the barren winter landscape "lovely as ever," noting the floors of stores and saloons were covered every night by sleeping men taking shelter from the bitter cold. He described these desperate prospectors as "nearly every man being a millionaire—in his own opinion."[181]

Daly stayed in central Nevada for about a year and a half and may have become a mine foreman. In June 1870, the federal census listed him as a resident of Hamilton, Nevada.[182] Meanwhile, John and Anna O'Farrell began to follow Daly instead of the other way around. Their youngest son, Marcus O'Farrell, was born in California around 1869, but the 1870 census records the family as residents of Virginia City where they remained until at least 1880. They later joined Daly in Montana.[183]

Mineral Hill, where a smelter began operating in 1869, was about fifty miles from White Pine. The camp was home to another Irishman and lifelong friend of Daly's: Jeremiah Kelley (1841–1901). Both men worked the Comstock, and Kelley became a mine manager at Mineral Hill. Writing in the 1950s, Isaac Marcosson stated that Daly worked at Mineral Hill as well as White Pine, though there is little other evidence Daly lived there. Marcosson's source was probably Jeremiah's son Cornelius "Con" Kelley (1875–1957), who ultimately became president and chairman of the board of the Anaconda Company. The Kelley family came to Butte in 1881, where young Con quietly listened when Daly and his father spent casual evenings swapping tales of Nevada.[184]

The Central Nevada boom was short-lived. By 1870, people were moving on. Daly was in Utah by autumn.[185] There, he met the Walker brothers—and his future wife.

5

THE BOSS IRISHMAN

Marcus Daly's arrival in Utah began the prime years of his mining career. No longer a footloose young man with "a grub stake and a prospector's kit," Daly finally ran mining operations in Utah, putting into practice lessons he had learned over the preceding decade. He married, started a family, became a naturalized American citizen, and patented his first mining claims. Daly was a natural leader in Utah's rowdy mining camps, noted for their significant Irish Catholic population. Utah launched him as a "boss Irishman," descendant of the *ceann fine*, a role he developed to its fullest in Montana.[186]

Most of Utah Territory's white settlers focused on agriculture and were members of the Church of Jesus Christ of Latter-day Saints, then commonly called Mormons. They migrated west, having survived significant persecution for their nontraditional form of Christianity, which, until 1890, included polygamy. As the Mormons set up farms and ranches, the United States government added a military presence, ostensibly protecting settlers from Native tribes but also keeping an eye on the Latter-day Saints, who were viewed with prejudice and suspicion by mainstream society. Some soldiers turned to mining and uncovered Utah's silver riches.

Unlike freewheeling Nevada, Utah had an uneasy relationship with work and play. Gambling was outlawed, but Mormon Church president Brigham Young, like countless moral reformers before and since, inveighed against gambling and horse racing often enough to confirm their popularity. Meanwhile, military outposts and Daly's world—the mining camps—embraced both.[187]

Bridging these worlds were the Walker brothers of Salt Lake City, four savvy young businessmen with interests in mercantilism, banking, and by 1870, silver. They hired Daly to run their mines and launched him on the trajectory that led to Montana Territory.

TRAVELERS AND TRADERS

The land between South Pass in present-day Wyoming and Utah's Great Salt Lake was a crossroads and trading area. Native people of many tribes met at well-established Shoshone camps to exchange trade goods and fine horses. European-American fur trappers joined the mix when the Rocky Mountain Fur Company set up the Green River Rendezvous in 1825.[188]

To the northwest, the Hudson Bay Company founded Fort Hall in 1834 on the Snake River in present-day Idaho. By the late 1840s, it was a stop where westward-bound travelers resupplied before making the crucial decision of whether to continue on the Oregon Trail or go to California. Fort Hall

The Shoshone people set up trading camps between South Pass and the Great Salt Lake. Eastern Shoshone Village, Wind River Mountains, Wyoming, 1870. *Utah State Historical Society.*

also became a station along the north–south Montana Trail, a freight road running from the Great Salt Lake over Monida Pass into Montana.[189] That route brought Daly to Butte in 1876.

THE WALKER BROTHERS

Utah's white settlement began in earnest when Brigham Young's Vanguard Company of Mormon pioneers came to the Salt Lake Valley in 1847. The Latter-day Saints' Perpetual Emigration Fund even drew people from overseas by offering reduced ship fares, bringing converts to Utah Territory's "Kingdom of Zion." Roughly eighty-six thousand white people had settled there by the time Daly arrived in 1870.[190]

These migrants included Matthew Walker Sr., a merchant from Yorkshire, England, and his innkeeper wife, the former Mercy Long (1805–1863). By 1847, they were modestly wealthy and owned a small English estate, but when their investments in shaky railroad stocks collapsed, they lost almost everything they owned. Matthew Walker met an auctioneer who was a Mormon, learned of the Perpetual Emigration Fund, and dreamed of a clean start in America. The family converted to Mormonism and left England in 1850.[191]

The cheap emigrant ships were overcrowded with inadequate food and water. Matthew contracted tuberculosis and only made it as far as St. Louis, where he died in June 1851. Matthew and Mercy's two daughters died of cholera six weeks later.

The three teenaged Walker boys, Samuel Sharp (1834–1887), Joseph Robinson (1836–1901), and David Frederick (1838–1910), known by their middle names Sharp, Rob, and Fred, respectively, had to support their mother and six-year-old brother, Matthew Jr. (1845–1916). In these hard times, second-born Rob Walker developed the business savvy and leadership that made him the de facto head of the family.[192]

Mercy and the boys joined a Utah-bound Mormon pioneer train in 1852. Settling in Salt Lake City, their next struggle sowed the seeds of their later split with the Latter-day Saints. Hungry and cold, Rob and Fred helped build the Mormon temple during their first desperate winter and were enraged to be paid nothing; church officials explained that labor was their tithe in lieu of paying 10 percent of their income to the church. Eventually, Rob began hauling freight, and Fred found work as a store clerk. Sharp Walker obtained a twenty-acre allotment and began farming.[193]

Left to right: Samuel Sharp Walker, Joseph Robinson Walker, David Frederick Walker, and Matthew Walker Jr. *Artist unknown.*

In 1856, Rob Walker visited the Washoe with trade goods, took pack mules into California, and developed business connections on the coast. California gold tempted the boys to leave Utah, but their mother urged them to stay. Mercy Walker's caution and business sense helped them accumulate a respectable fortune, but they also became risk-adverse and later ignored Marcus Daly's advice on two occasions, each time costing them a shot at a stratospheric fortune that went instead to the Hearst-Haggin-Tevis syndicate.[194]

In 1857, during the boondoggle known as the Utah War, the Walkers opened their first drygoods store near the military outpost of Camp Floyd at Fairfield, Utah. They purchased a large safe to hold their profits, and it soon safeguarded the valuables of others—their first bank in all but name. Matt Jr., age fourteen, joined the family business as the bank teller and bookkeeper, the first step to his adult career as president of the Walker Brothers Bank.

In 1860, they opened a second store in downtown Salt Lake City, serving customers from both Mormon and "gentile" (non-Mormon) ranks. Their big break came in 1861, when Camp Floyd closed and the quartermaster unloaded a $4 million inventory of surplus goods for $100,000. The Walkers

Walker Brothers Store, Salt Lake City, Utah Territory. *NYPL.*

bought $20,000 worth. Reselling their windfall at a significant profit, the Walkers, all under the age of thirty, became the second-wealthiest family in Utah.[195]

Brigham Young noticed their failure to tithe 10 percent of their profits to the church. He sent in a bishop to demand they pay up. Recalling their "tithe" of unpaid labor on the Temple, they instead handed over their regular $500 donation to the Perpetual Emigration Fund. Young issued an ultimatum that they tithe fully or be cut off from the church. Calling his bluff, they allegedly replied, "Go ahead and cut off."[196]

Incensed, Young convened a conclave, excommunicated them, and urged "all good Mormons" to spurn Walker Brothers and Company. But now gentiles in the eyes of the Mormon Church, the Walkers quickly regrouped, openly adding high-profit items such as alcohol and tobacco to their inventory. They still had the largest safe in town, and many "good Mormons" continued to patronize them, sneaking in the back door and exiting with purchases wrapped in unmarked brown paper.[197]

PROSPECTING SOLDIERS

Utah's mining boom began courtesy of the Third California Volunteer Infantry Regiment, which arrived in 1862. The military was officially protecting overland mail and telegraph lines from "Indian attacks," but they set up Camp Douglas on high ground overlooking Salt Lake City. Brigham Young declared the Civil War to be God's punishment of a sinful nation, and the federal government questioned the loyalties of the Latter-day Saints. The regiment's Irish-born commander Colonel Patrick Edward Connor (circa 1820–1892) held a personal anti-Mormon animus, calling them "a community of traitors, murderers, fanatics and whores."[198]

The regiment's first—and virtually only—military operation was the brutal January 29, 1863 Massacre at Boa Ogoi, also called the Bear River Massacre. On the pretext of protecting settlers, the regiment attacked a civilian Northwestern Shoshone winter camp near present-day Preston, Idaho. They killed nearly five hundred men, women, and children, the largest death toll of Native people in a single attack in the history of the American West.[199]

Thereafter, the troops had little to do. Many were California miners and—with Connor's approval—spent their idle hours prospecting. Acting on a tip from local loggers, some soldiers found silver in Bingham Canyon, twenty-five miles from Salt Lake City. In 1864, they struck gold. Connor quickly staked his own claims, organized the West Mountain Quartz Mining District, and was dubbed the "father of Utah mining."[200]

Soon, the Utah rush was on. The Walkers already had military supply contracts, but their business soon expanded to include prospectors who needed supplies and a safe place to keep their wealth. Buying a larger safe and expanding into commercial loans, they became true bankers. By 1865, they were millionaires.[201]

DALY TO THE WASATCH

Brigham Young, fed up with price gouging of the Walkers and other gentiles, brought Mormon merchants together in 1868 under the umbrella of ZCMI, the Zion Cooperative Mercantile Institute. ZCMI undercut the Walkers, whose store sales plummeted. They also knew the transcontinental railroad would soon arrive, increasing the supply of drygoods and further dropping prices. Freight and banking kept them solvent, but the Walkers had to diversify.[202]

Rob Walker's freight hauling business allowed him to put his thumb on mining's pulse. He noticed that the silver coming out of Little Cottonwood Canyon in the Wasatch Range made a boomtown called Alta hum with activity.[203]

Golden spike ceremony joining the Central Pacific and Union Pacific Railroads, Promontory Summit, Utah Territory, May 10, 1869. *Wikimedia Commons.*

In 1868, prospectors at Alta's Emma mine uncovered a vein of lead-carbonate ore containing more silver than the average assay on the Comstock—just as they ran out of capital. Seeing as sure a thing as ever occurred in mining, the Walkers stepped in with $30,000, purchased a 25 percent share in the operation, and formed the Emma Silver Mining Company of Utah.[204]

Just as Haggin and Tevis needed Hearst a decade earlier, the Walkers needed a trustworthy connection who knew the world underground. With silver mines playing out in Central Nevada, it was no surprise that Marcus Daly came to Utah. It is unclear if he moved on his own initiative or if he was recruited. There are two stories of how Daly came to the attention of the Walkers. One is that George Hearst recommended him. The better documented account says that "Jack" MacMaster*, another Comstock veteran, encouraged Daly to come to Utah and recommended him to the Walkers.[205]

---

* MacMaster's first name varies: Jack, John, and Thomas all seem to refer to the same person.

"General View of Emma Mine," circa 1870. *LOC.*

In any case, Daly became foreman of the Emma. As the shaft deepened, the vein widened from four to thirty-five feet. The Emma produced a $200,000 profit by the end of 1870 and $500,000 in 1871.[206]

This was where Daly revealed that, like Hearst, he had a "nose for ore." He had worked the boom-bust cycles of Nevada's Comstock and observed firsthand the rapid rise and fall of the diggings at White Pine. As his miners developed the Emma, Daly suspected it was not a property for the long haul. In 1871, he recommended the Walkers sell, and they did. Speculators snapped up the property at its peak, only to see it become worthless within two years. Meanwhile, the Walkers quietly acquired clear title to most of the federal land under the town of Alta and were reselling city lots to people who had already built homes and businesses there. As the dust settled, they banked another million and gained considerable faith in Marcus Daly.[207]

The exchange of knowledge flowed both directions. Daly observed the Walkers and, like them, diversified his investments. At Daly's death in 1900, his Montana assets not only included Amalgamated Copper stock and mining claims but also water rights and land in at least eight counties; city lots in Anaconda, Butte, Hamilton, and Missoula; a lumber mill; the Butte, Anaconda & Pacific Railroad (which ran from Butte to Garrison, Montana); two banks; and the Bitter Root Stock Farm.[208]

Ophir and the Ontario

Having disposed of the Emma, the Walkers shifted their attention—and Daly—to the Oquirrh Mountains south of the Great Salt Lake, home to Tooele County's Ophir Mining district. They already had claims in the area, including a partnership with Patrick Connor in a mine called Silveropolis.[209]

At Ophir, the Walkers made Daly the superintendent of their entire Mountain Tiger group of mines. He brought the diggings into full production, and in October 1871, the *Salt Lake Daily Review* said of Daly, "He is worth a mine himself to the owners." By 1872, the Walkers not only controlled multiple mines and Ophir's freight business, but they also ran the fifteen-stamp Pioneer Mill, the first to operate in Utah. Daly's miners sent the mill ten tons of high-grade silver chloride ore each day.[210]

Daly remained alert for additional prospects. In 1872, he heard of a mine in Ontario Gulch, near present-day Park City. Traveling there with Rob Walker, the two men basically saw a "little hole in the ground." Looking at the area with a miner's eye, Daly felt it had promise. But based on "ore in sight" and always cautious, the Walkers passed on the property.[211] It was one of their few strategic blunders.

Meanwhile, George Hearst was also looking for new prospects. He was in Utah on July 18, 1872, and may have stayed until November. Newspapers noted Hearst's family was with him, though Phoebe took a train back to San Francisco on August 24.[212]

R.C. Chambers in the Ontario Mine office, circa 1900. *Park City Historical Society and Museum.*

Hearst ran into Daly near present-day Park City at Lake Flat, also known as Bonanza Flat. Having given the Walkers their shot, Daly mentioned the Ontario to Hearst, who assayed an ore sample. Seeing the results, Hearst brought in R.C. Chambers (1832–1901), his right-hand man in Nevada, to handle negotiations. After a certain amount of subterfuge to thwart the prospectors' ever-increasing asking price, on August 26, 1872, newspapers announced that Hearst bought the claim for $27,000. He named Chambers his mining superintendent. In December, Hearst obtained a patent, and by January 1874, the Hearst-Haggin-Tevis syndicate owned the property. The Ontario became the richest single silver mine in Utah, producing total profits of at least $14 million.[213]

Chambers and Daly were lifetime friends. Chambers settled in Utah, serving in the state legislature, but invested heavily in Montana. In 1882, he built Butte's Chambers Block, and then he and Daly became partners in the bank it housed: Hoge, Brownlee, and Company.[214]

Legal Matters

Western mining was revolutionized by a major change in federal law: the General Mining Act of May 10, 1872, commonly called the 1872 Mining Law. Prior to 1872, claims were governed by a mishmash of local laws while legal title to the ground remained with the federal government. The General Mining Act not only standardized laws across the West, but it prioritized mining as the "highest and best use" of the public domain. Under the act, prospectors could file claims and hold them as long as they provided evidence of "representing"—performing a minimal amount of work each year. If the claim proved lucrative, a claimant could file for a patent to obtain permanent title from the U.S. government, granting ownership of both the surface land and underground minerals for a nominal fee of $2.50 to $5.00 an acre.[215]

Daly staked some claims himself. But to patent them, he ran into an obstacle: he wasn't a U.S. citizen. It is unclear why Daly hadn't obtained his citizenship after nearly two decades in America—it was simple at the time. Applicants declared before a court of record their "bona fide intention" to become a citizen of the United States. After five years, applicants returned to court with two witnesses to swear to their good character, took the oath of allegiance, and were granted citizenship. It is not known when Daly filed his initial declaration, but he finalized matters in Utah. On April 15, 1874, he was granted citizenship in Salt Lake City.[216]

The two witnesses to Daly's "good character" give insights into Daly's social circle. Like Daly, they were veterans of the Comstock, became active in Utah's Irish Catholic community, and were known for their wit and rough humor.

Irish-born P.H. "Pat" Lannan (or Launan) (1839–1925) was called a "character"—even in his obituary. He was a cattle buyer who reached the Comstock by 1863; there, he served as justice of the peace. In Utah, he won a federal lawsuit against Brigham Young, who sued him for setting up a meat market without the consent of ZCMI. Lannan bought the *Salt Lake Tribune* in 1883. He retired to Los Angeles, living at the prestigious Jonathan Club for the final fifteen years of his life.

New York–born Lemuel Ulysses "Lem" Colbath (1832–1908) was a Comstock miner, noted as a wag in the local papers. He reached Utah in 1872 and became the superintendent of the Vallejo Mine, near the Emma. He went on to work for R.C. Chambers at the Ontario, described as Chambers' "right hand man."[217]

Citizenship in hand, Daly moved quickly. By 1875, he patented multiple claims but then learned some hard lessons. His ventures in the Blue Ledge district by Park City were unsuccessful. He owned the Poorman's mine in Ophir in partnership with the Walkers, and it endured disaster. A freak snowstorm in March 1876 produced an avalanche that wiped out the mining equipment and swept away the boardinghouse; three men died. Daly, the boss of the operation, directed over 150 people in a search for their remains.[218]

MARGARET

Though Daly's difficulties stung, his path through Utah held more good than bad, particularly in his personal life.

An Ohio farm family settled in Ophir: Zenas Evans, his wife, Margaret Holmes Evans, and their six children.* Evans reached Utah in 1866 or 1867. He became a partner in Latimer, Taylor and Company, where he ran a sawmill with a partner, Charles Decker, while Thomas Latimer and George Taylor manufactured flooring, sashes, and doors. An 1868 fire destroyed the company's works in Salt Lake City, and thereafter, Latimer and Taylor dropped their partners. Evans rebuilt his finances; the 1870 census listed him with his family in Atlantic City, Wyoming, a small mining town in Sweetwater County near South Pass, the site of a short-lived gold rush. There, Evans identified himself as a miner.[219]

Margaret Daly, circa 1900.
Daly Mansion.

When Wyoming's boom played out, the family returned to Utah and the lumber business. Evans set up Ophir's first sawmill, and the city directory listed him as a millwright. Timber was in high demand: underground works used vast quantities of wood to support the diggings, while buildings in the boomtown went up at a rapid pace.[220]

Evans also invested in various mines. He owned shares in the Walkers' Mountain Tiger group and was a partner in the "Green Chloride" mines, one of which was named the Hattie Evans, presumably after his youngest daughter.[221]

---

* The spelling of Zenas Erastus Evans's name used herein is the most common spelling. Variants include Z.E., Enos, Zenos, Zenes, Zenith, and Zenns.

The life-size *Stabat Mater* or "Calvary" at St. Mary's Church, Crosserlough Parish, donated by Daly in 1894. *Mary O'Reilly.*

Margaret Price Evans (1853–1941), the family's eldest daughter, had nerves of steel. Some accounts describe her eye for numbers and speculate that she kept her father's books. One day, Zenas Evans joined Daly to inspect a mine for a potential timber order, and Margaret came along. Picking her way across irregular terrain in the dark, damp, treacherous diggings, she slipped on an incline, and Daly caught her. As the family tale went, she literally "fell into his arms."[222] Romance blossomed.

Marcus and Margaret's wedding was held in the living room of Rob Walker's mansion in Salt Lake City on September 20, 1872. It was an ideal setting: Daly was Catholic, Margaret identified as Episcopalian, and the Walkers had become an ecumenical family. Molly Gerard stated, "I think George Hearst was at the wedding, as I have some silver that Mr. Hearst gave them." That said, R.C. Chambers was there and gave a firsthand account in a 1900 interview, but he did not mention that Hearst attended. Chambers may have delivered the gift on behalf of his boss. It is undetermined if Hearst was in town. He purchased the Ontario about a month earlier, but on September 18, the Salt Lake City Post Office nagged him to pick up his mail at general delivery.[223]

According to County Cavan oral history, Daly's mother was unhappy that he married a Protestant, and in a fit of pique, she disowned him, even refusing to accept the remittances he sent to her. In turn, when he visited Ireland—perhaps the same trip that gave rise to the story about Cummings and his pigs—he allegedly refused to visit his mother. Nonetheless, in 1894, Daly provided funds for the Calvary sculpture at St. Mary's Church in Crosserlough Parish. It included a plaque acknowledging his gift, adding, "Pray for the souls of his deceased parents."[224]

Daly's Utah years may have been the happiest of his life. Marcus and Margaret's first two children were born there: Margaret Augusta Daly (called "Maggie" when young and "Madge" when grown) arrived in 1873. Molly was born on January 13, 1876. A reporter for the *Utah Weekly Miner* wrote on January 24, "Our old friend Mark Daly, in charge of Walker Bros. cluster of mines, walks the mountains 'like a thing of life,' as hearty as a buck and as happy as a lord."[225]

LEADERSHIP

Using the word *lord* to describe Daly suggests he first became a "boss Irishman" in Utah, consciously or otherwise taking the mantle held by Irish chieftains, the *ceann fine* of old. People from Ireland brought their cultural assumptions to the mining camps of the American Rockies, including their understanding of leadership.[226] Daly lived the reality that power and responsibility went together. Just two months after he felt the joy of Molly's birth, he was directing men to dig into snowbanks at the Poorman's Mining Camp, searching for bodies of the dead.

Even before the avalanche at the Poorman's, Daly understood that mining injuries were inevitable and deaths far too common. Medical care was crucial. To get it, he teamed up with a charismatic young priest whose energy and drive resembled that of Daly himself: Father Lawrence Scanlan (1843–1915).

The Irish-dominated mining camps held most of Utah's Catholic population. Their hazardous work mixed raw courage

Father Lawrence Scanlan. *Utah State Historical Society.*

with superstition and appeals to the almighty for protection. Itinerant priests made rounds of the camps, performing mass and ministering to the flock. Scanlan, originally from County Tipperary, reached Utah in 1873. The vigorous priest was described as "adored by the miners in the camps which he visited. He was not afraid to soil his clothes by going down the shafts, encouraging the men, bringing them the realization that he was indeed their shepherd."[227] Scanlan later became the first Catholic bishop of Salt Lake City.

While a superintendent at Ophir, Daly personally urged Scanlan to recruit some Sisters of the Holy Cross to come to Utah to start a hospital. Several sisters, all trained nurses, soon arrived, and Holy Cross Hospital in Salt Lake City opened in 1875. Daly's connections to the world of medicine continued in Montana, where he supported hospitals, financed pharmacies, and built a state-of-the-art veterinary hospital at the Bitter Root Stock Farm for his animals. After his death, Margaret Daly established the Marcus Daly Memorial Hospital in Hamilton, Montana.[228]

The Next Stage

In 1876, Daly made his most significant journey since boarding a ship to America twenty years earlier.

Montana's gold rush began in 1862, but in 1875, a stagnant gold camp called Butte City reawakened to the lure of silver. Increasing amounts of ore from Montana Territory began appearing at the transcontinental railhead at Corinne, Utah.[229]

One account states the Walkers became interested in Butte when a former Utah resident, Rolla Butcher, bought supplies from them and paid in concentrated ore. But more likely, Rob Walker noticed when several freight shipments from Butte's Late Acquisition mine arrived in June 1876, totaling about eighty-five tons of silver ore.[230]

Intrigued, the Walkers sent Daly north. He took the Utah and Northern Railroad to its northern terminus at Franklin, Idaho. From there, he took a stagecoach to Butte City.[231] The fortunes of both man and community were soon to change in a dramatic fashion.

BUTTE CITY AND THE ALICE

I shall start for Montana Tuesday.
The stage was held up three times last week. Here's hoping I have better luck.
—Daly [232]

In the summer of 1876, Daly stepped off a stagecoach in Butte City, Montana Territory. He arrived well after the placer gold operations of the 1860s were supplanted by underground lode mines that produced silver. Those who made their fortunes "mining the miners," such as cattle king Conrad Kohrs and bankers W.A. Clark and S.E. Larabie, were well established.

When Daly came to Montana, he was thirty-four years old, in the prime of his life, a seasoned miner and competent manager. His knowledge of geology and engineering was learned from the ground up. Energetic, of medium height, but "large-framed, large brained, and brawny-muscled," Daly radiated the essence of early Butte, described by historian Michael Malone as "the democratic, hairy-chested mining camp."[233]

Later tales claimed Daly snuck into town in disguise, surreptitiously taking a mining job in order to scout prospects. He personally debunked that story in an 1895 interview but added, "I know many a good man who has come into Butte packing his blankets. It would be perfectly satisfactory to me if I had came into town that way." In 1876, gossip was buzzing. Nephi Packard of the Late Acquisition mine shared letters from his brother in Utah with the *Butte Miner*, and on July 22, 1876, the paper reported that "one of the Walker

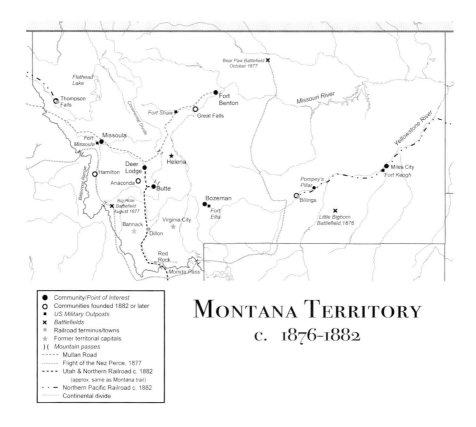

MONTANA TERRITORY
c. 1876-1882

- ● Community/Point of Interest
- ○ Communities founded 1882 or later
- ■ US Military Outposts
- ✕ Battlefields
- ▪ Railroad terminus/towns
- ★ Former territorial capitals
-)(Mountain passes
- ----- Mullan Road
- ·········· Flight of the Nez Perce, 1877
- - - - Utah & Northern Railroad c. 1882
  (approx. same as Montana trail)
- · · — Northern Pacific Railroad c. 1882
- ·········· Continental divide

bros." planned to visit the silver camp. The only subterfuge was sending an agent—Daly.[234]

The exact date he arrived is not known. On August 25, 1876, the *New North-West* reported his departure, commenting, "Daly, a western miner of experience and a gentleman of excellent sense, who has been looking around the quartz camps for some time, left by coach for Idaho yesterday and we trust will see it to his interest to come back some day and take a hand at mining in Montana."[235]

When the Walkers purchased the Alice mine, Daly became both a minority shareholder and superintendent. The Alice made Daly well-off, and he rooted firmly in Montana. Given that his employers lived four hundred miles away, he had a free rein in management and was the leader on the ground to whom the workers owed their jobs and their loyalty.

Life in Butte was not only work and toil. It was a lively place, and Daly was active in the community. Clubs and committees were as important as ore and stamp mills to Daly's plans, allowing him to befriend allies—and keep an eye on his competition. A brand-new racetrack drew several of Butte's—and Montana's—future political players.

TRADERS AND CATTLE KINGS

Conrad Kohrs. *Leeson, 557.*

Deer Lodge, forty miles northwest of present-day Butte, was the county seat of a region that today encompasses Powell, Granite, Deer Lodge, and Silver Bow Counties. Originally a Native trading area, in the 1860s, it became a hotbed for raising livestock to feed hungry miners, and the trader who bridged the Native and white worlds was Johnny Grant (1831–1907).[236]

Grant came west as a teenager to live with his father, Fort Hall's agent Richard Grant. They grew wealthy by trading cash-poor pioneers two head of trail-worn livestock for one animal that was sound and rested, often drawn from those purchased from the previous year's desperate travelers. Young Johnny also exchanged travelers' thin, exhausted, but finely bred horses for hardy local mustangs.[237]

Eventually, Johnny Grant left Fort Hall, settling permanently in the Deer Lodge Valley in 1859 with horses, cattle—and multiple Native wives. He owned over one thousand head of cattle in 1862, when prospectors struck gold on Grasshopper Creek. He struck it rich selling beef to hungry gold-seekers. Along the way, he befriended and bankrolled a middleman: the hardworking butcher and cattle broker Conrad Kohrs. As white settlement made life increasingly uncomfortable for Grant and his polygamous, multiracial family, he moved to Canada in 1866 and sold his ranch to Kohrs.[238]

Kohrs's cattle empire grew until he controlled much of Montana's beef industry. His half-brother John Bielenberg arrived in 1864, taking charge of the equestrian side of the business. Marcus Daly met Kohrs and Bielenberg in 1877. The men became friends—and friendly rivals at the track. As Daly became Montana's racing king as well as a copper king, Kohrs explained, "Up to 1893 and 1894, John Bielenberg's colts had always been fortunate enough to beat the colts of Marcus Daly, but after 1894, we were not so successful."[239]

THE INVENTOR

Pioneers named one Deer Lodge Valley settlement Racetrack after a flat straightaway that was used for Native intertribal competition. White settlers soon staked out oval tracks. One track was owned by another of Kohrs's half-brothers, Nick Bielenberg, but the best known was Olin's Course. Owned by machinist and inventor Giles Olin (1818–1877), the fine one-mile oval was built in 1869, complete with a judges' stand and bleachers.[240]

Olin, originally a blacksmith, was a colorful figure. He "joined the stampede" in the winter of 1864–65 to a short-lived gold camp called Blackfoot (north of present-day Avon, Montana), where he lost both feet to frostbite. After the amputations, he moved about on protheses he designed himself, aided by canes. For longer distances, he rode a donkey until "poor Jack" died in 1873; then he used a dogcart pulled by a pair of Newfoundlands.[241]

The racetrack was only the first of Olin's projects. Ever curious and endlessly tinkering, in 1871, he constructed a commercial greenhouse in Deer Lodge, with beds warmed by steam heat from buried pipes. He patented a stamp mill design and an engine for propelling canal boats in 1873, then he was a machinist in Helena in 1874–75.[242]

Olin's final act was in Butte. In the spring of 1876, just prior to Daly's arrival, he built a Cornish jig on Silver Bow Creek. It used pulsating water to separate ore from gangue and was Montana's first successful copper concentrator. Each day, it reduced two tons of crude rock down to one ton of ore. On August 25, 1876, the same day the *New North-West* reported Daly's departure, the paper described Olin's operation, commenting it was "of great benefit to the miners."[243]

Olin died of "apoplexy" in July 1877, eulogized as "a well-educated gentleman and an esteemed citizen."[244] Just as Johnny Grant bridged the transition from Native to white culture and Conrad Kohrs developed Montana's livestock industry, Giles Olin's eclectic projects followed Montana's economy as it shifted toward industrial mining.

Butte City

In 1856, explorer Caleb Irvine passed through the Summit Valley at the foot of the Continental Divide. There, he noted old signs of mining by unknown parties. The area was ignored until 1864, when a group of prospectors found color "upon a bend of the stream…the glistening waters of the 'silver bow' etched in a shimmering sheen." Soon, the gold camp of Silver Bow sprung up. As the usual flood of miners arrived, tents and shanties extended seven miles up Silver Bow Creek toward a distinct formation, the "Big Butte," where another camp formed, optimistically named Butte City, or simply "Butte." There, water was scarce for placer mining, so some miners looked at the quartz lodes in the hills, including a pre-existing hole in the ground, later named the Original—possibly the diggings noted by Irvine.[245]

By 1866, Butte City was described by historian Harry Freeman as a wild camp where "no man was safe without a brace of revolvers in his belt and a Bowie knife tucked into his bootleg." As the gold played out, a few hardy souls stayed on, working quartz leads rich in silver. Some were veterans of the Comstock. They knew silver ore was more complicated and expensive to reduce than gold, yet ever-optimistic, they built a smelter in 1866 and then a five-stamp mill and a second smelting furnace in 1868. All were financial failures.[246]

Roadside marker near Rocker, Montana, commemorating the 1864 gold discovery in Silver Bow Creek. *Wahler.*

Freight wagons near Fort Benton, Montana. *Image:* Wagon Boss, *C.M. Russell, 1909.*

Another problem was geography: until the railroad arrived, pack trains and freight wagons had only two options to get ore from the Butte Hill to a transportation hub. The first route went north about two hundred miles to Fort Benton, the most inland steamboat port in America. The other option, as railroads inched toward Promontory Summit, went south about four hundred miles to Utah's railheads and refining works. With poor transportation, limited processing capacity, and insufficient capital, Butte's population fell from about 500 in 1867 to 241 in 1870.[247]

The 1872 Mining Law offered little immediate relief to Butte. For one thing, there was plenty of silver elsewhere: Mackay struck the Comstock's Big Bonanza in March 1873, while in Utah, Hearst's Ontario and the Walkers' Ophir mines were ongoing concerns. Western mining interests also discovered they had little control over international finance when the Panic of 1873 crashed the price of silver. With only one saloon and fifty or sixty souls left by 1874, Butte City was on the cusp of becoming a ghost town.[248]

Bill Farlin got credit for saving Butte and kick-starting a silver rush. He had abandoned Montana for better prospects, but when he left, he took ore samples with him. In 1874, he obtained reliable assays, discovering his ore was rich in silver and copper. He returned to Butte that October and quietly bided his time. He knew the 1872 Mining Law contained a provision that anyone who went for one year without "representing" their claim forfeited it unless an exception applied. Furthermore, at the stroke of midnight, January

1, 1875, all exceptions granting extra time expired, leaving many claims ripe for the taking. The night of December 31–January 1, Farlin staked, posted notice, and thus "relocated" at least fifteen claims. He trekked to Deer Lodge later, recording the first of these claims on January 14, 1875.[249]

While Farlin looked to silver, Billy Parks put Butte copper on the map at the Parrott lode. He invested in the failed 1866 smelter, then spent years of mostly solo work digging a shaft, using a hand-cranked windlass and bucket made from half a whiskey keg. His fellow miners considered him a crackpot. But when Parks reached 150 feet, he hit a 4-foot-wide vein of "copper glace"—chalcocite—an iridescent gray ore that glistened in Parks's candlelight. On October 29, 1875, the *New North-West* announced, "This claim yields the best copper ore in the camp." In 1876, Parks brought a ton of ore daily to Olin's concentrator. Finally considered a genius instead of a fool, Parks sold his claim for between $10,000 and $30,000 and retired to a quiet life in Madison County. His claim, later known as Parrot Number One ("Parrot" and "Parrott" are both used in various records), produced $1 million worth of copper.[250]

By the end of 1876, Butte's population rebounded to one thousand.[251] Most of all, investors were finally paying attention.

The Bankers

Mining carried great financial risks. Promising leads petered out, shipments were vulnerable to outlaws prowling the primitive roads, and prices were at the mercy of factors far beyond Montana Territory.

Butte miners also faced a perplexing situation: silver ore seemed to play out at the water table. Later, the Walker brothers' mining expert, John Clayton, theorized that water was oxidizing and leaching out valuable minerals. He suspected—correctly—that once the diggings went lower, good ore would return. However, dropping shafts below the water table meant spending money upfront digging sumps to gather water, installing pumps to remove it, and obtaining wood or coal to heat the boilers to produce the steam that powered the pumps.[252]

Prospectors needed partnerships and outside capital. Those with money scrambled for control of promising claims, and the original discoverers sometimes went from mine owner to minion in the process. At the front of the pack of local investors was the brilliant and complicated man who became part of Daly's extended family and his archrival: William Andrews "W.A." Clark (1839–1925).

> *To look at* [Clark] *and his diminutive stature, rather delicate physique and his nervous manner, you could never think that such a man could have endured for a generation the sufferings and vicissitudes of frontier life. And yet, look into that eye and you see a soul of iron, a will as resolute as adamant.*
> —*P.A. O'Farrell*[253]

Clark was born in Pennsylvania, descended from Scots-Irish Presbyterian emigrants from County Tyrone in Ulster. Described by Joseph Kinsey Howard as "a tight white starched little man," Clark taught school and studied law before the lure of gold—and a desire to avoid Civil War drafts—brought him west in 1862. He moved from Colorado to Bannack, Montana, in 1863 and, within a year, started a freight business, transporting mail and buying goods that he resold at premium prices.[254]

Clark mastered how to mine the miners. "Never a dollar got away from him that didn't come back stuck to another," explained Howard. Clark bought tobacco at $1.50 a pound in Boise, Idaho, and sold it for $5.00 in Helena. With his grasp of supply and demand, he sold flour in the winter of 1864–65 for an eye-popping $1.00 to $1.50 a pound—over $20.00 today. Even though it was the height of the vigilante era, no one hanged him for highway robbery. Clark's best-known exploit was transporting eggs from Salt Lake City to Montana one December, counting on them to freeze so they would arrive intact. He sold them to the saloons, and with a splash of brandy, everyone celebrated the holidays with Tom and Jerrys.[255]

Like the Walkers, Clark's freight hauling soon led to storefronts and a bank. He partnered with merchant Robert Donnell and assayer Samuel Edward "Ed" Larabie (1845–1914), opening the Deer Lodge Bank of Donnell, Clark and Larabie in 1869. Paid in gold dust, by 1873, they sent over $1.5 million in gold a year to the Philadelphia Mint.[256]

Larabie was a horse aficionado who often took livestock as collateral for agricultural loans. His brother Charles X. Larrabee

William Andrews Clark, circa 1905. *LOC.*

A portion of a stamp mill, World Museum of Mining. *Wahler.*

(1843–1914) reached Montana in 1875, bringing along a string of fine Morgan horses.* Larabie's Willow Run Stock Farm soon bred harness trotters and Thoroughbreds, eventually owning several East Coast champions.[257]

Meanwhile, Clark focused on Butte, taking mining claims as loan collateral. By 1872, he was foreclosing on claims at a steady pace and using his knowledge of the market to buy others on the cheap. Clark's fledgling empire soon included the Original, Colusa, Gambetta, and Mountain Chief mines. In 1877, Clark opened a Butte branch of Donnell, Clark, and Larabie.[258]

Unlike Haggin and Tevis, who partnered with Hearst for mining expertise, or the Walkers, who hired Daly, Clark became his own expert. He went east in the winter of 1872–73 to study at the School of Mines at Columbia University. Bringing ore to assay, he confirmed his mines were rich in copper, even if he could not yet reduce it. In the meantime, Clark dove into the reviving silver rush in 1875. He added more mines to his collection, including a silver property called the Moulton, located high above Butte on the Rainbow lode, named for the silver-bearing outcrop that ran across a hill high above town.[259]

Clark's most important investment at the time was a loan to Bill Farlin, who built the silver-processing Dexter stamp mill and refinery. It opened on June 1, 1876, with Clark's brother J. Ross serving as bookkeeper. Clark bought out Farlin in 1877 in a complex foreclosure action and gained control over much of the silver reduction in Butte.[260]

Samuel T. Hauser and Andrew Jackson "A.J." Davis were the first bankers to compete with Clark. After silver was discovered in 1865, Hauser built a smelter in 1866 at Argenta in Beaverhead County. Then he settled in Helena, shifted to banking, and partnered with Davis to open Butte's S.T. Hauser and Company Bank in 1877. Hauser later was one of the "big four" power players in Montana's Democratic Party, along with Clark, Daly, and railroad investor C.A. Broadwater. Davis invested in Butte's 1868 stamp mill and bought the Lexington silver mine about 1872. Selling it in 1881 made him one of Montana's earliest millionaires.[261]

None of these early bankers could invest on a scale that put Montana Territory on the map. They needed outside capital but hated to relinquish their independence. Davis summed up the local attitude; he was uninterested in having "a small interest with a large company."[262]

But as players gathered on the stage that was Butte, a stagecoach brought Marcus Daly to Montana for the next act.

---

* The brothers spelled their surnames differently.

THE ALICE

*Away to the north rimming the vista and pushing its rugged outlines up
scores of feet through the sharp ridges that have been upheld by the backbone
of quartz and granite traversing them is the old Rainbow lead, the most
northerly of the principal leads yet discovered and at the greatest altitude.*[263]

Farlin was not the only miner snapping up claims in January 1875. Rolla
Butcher (circa 1825–1882) was another. Virginia-born Butcher reached
California about 1860 and sold dry goods in Idaho by 1867. The 1870
census listed him as a resident of Corinne, Utah. Once in Butte, he saw
opportunities on the Rainbow lode. On January 2, 1875, Butcher located
the claim he named the Alice.[264]

Butcher had about a dozen claims, most owned in partnerships.
Sandwiched between his Alice and Rising Star claims was W.A. Clark's
Moulton. One of Butcher's partnerships, the Great Republic, profited
quickly when a fifteen-foot shaft uncovered a vein of silver chloride ore three
feet wide, "good for $100 a ton."[265]

In May 1875, Butcher sold a one-third interest in the Alice claim to Frank
Ramsdell. Ramsdell, later called "the father of quartz mining in Butte," sold
his interest in the Alice in December to Clark and Larabie for $600. After
that, it is unclear who worked the diggings: By June 1876, Butcher was busy
delivering issues of a brand-new newspaper, the *Butte Miner.*[266]

DALY ARRIVES

Alexander Graham Bell patented the telephone in March 1876, giving the
world another use for copper wire. But in Butte, even after Billy Parks's
copper strike, silver remained the talk of the town.

On June 13, 1876, the *Miner* reported that thirty tons of silver ore shipped
to the railhead at Corinne, Utah. On June 16, another forty tons went out.
On June 27, fifteen more tons headed to Salt Lake City. Most of it came
from the Late Acquisition mine.[267] The Utah press ignored these Montana
shipments when they arrived, roughly two weeks later, but that was not
surprising—plenty of silver moved through Utah. Further, people were
distracted: the nation's centennial celebration was on July 4, and a few days
later, blaring headlines reported General George Armstrong Custer's defeat

Butte City in 1875

Butte City, 1875–76, as it looked when Daly arrived. *BSB.*

at the June 25–26 Battle of the Little Bighorn. Only those observing the flow of freight—like Rob Walker—noticed that Butte had tons of expensive-to-ship silver and insufficient reduction capacity. The Walker brothers, with bank capital, a stamp mill, and a freight business, could overcome these challenges. They dispatched Daly to investigate.

After Daly's August 1876 visit, he returned to Butte a month later, along with Rob and Sharp Walker and their consultant, "Professor" John Clayton. By one account, the suggestion they look specifically at the Alice came from Nephi Packard, the gossipy co-owner of the Late Acquisition who tipped off the *Miner* about "one of the Walker bros." back in July.[268]

County records show "Joseph R. Walker"—Rob was the agent for Walker Brothers and Company—bought the Alice and several other claims on the Rainbow lode on September 28, 1876. The *Miner* was delighted: "[The Walkers'] identification with Butte is the most auspicious event in its history.…Mr. Daley [*sic*], who has had charge of their largest enterprises in Utah, will remain in Butte to superintend operations here."[269]

Several accounts assert that the Walkers' option on the Alice cost $25,000, which may reflect the sum that actually changed hands. But official records state that Rolla Butcher received $3,000 as consideration for his two-thirds share of the claim. Legally, an amount of "valuable consideration" had to change hands and be publicly acknowledged, but it was not necessarily the total purchase price. Clark demanded consideration of $3,500 for his and Larabie's one-third, and that sale was recorded on September 29. Including other claims, the Walkers' recorded consideration for their Butte investments in 1876 was between $8,000 and $11,000, though if larger sums were paid behind the scenes for the Alice, the same was probably true elsewhere.[270]

Rob and Sharp returned to Utah, planning to dismantle the Ophir Stamp Mill and ship it to Montana. Daly stayed on in Butte, hiring eight miners. He opened an assay office and brought in a chemist. On December 8, 1876, as agent for the Walkers, he filed for patents on the Alice and the Valdemere lodes. Daly had a 20 percent interest in the Alice.[271]

The purchase of the Alice in 1876 provides one of many theories for the origin of the Clark-Daly feud that tore apart the politics of Montana. The feud became public in 1888, when Clark sought election as Montana's territorial delegate to Congress. At the last minute, Daly, normally a Democrat, surreptitiously switched his support from Clark, the party's nominee, to Thomas Carter, the Republican. Carter won. Daly claimed legitimate business reasons for his decision, but Clark considered it a personal betrayal, and after that, the vicious rivalry played out in public.[272]

A 1933 account claimed the feud began when Clark's bank refused to honor a draft that Daly gave Rolla Butcher for the Alice. That particular tale has long been debunked because it does not match up with the historic record on multiple details, but its germ of truth may be that the sale sparked the feud. For one thing, Clark and Larabie received more consideration for their one-third share of the Alice than Butcher received for his two-thirds.[273] Clark's hard-nosed negotiation skills had to irk Daly.

Another theory holds their rivalry rose from a simple clash of personalities. Daly and Clark met within days of Daly's arrival in 1876, and Joseph Kinsey Howard believed the two men "hated each other on sight." They were striking opposites in nearly everything but ambition. Daly was a self-taught miner, a hearty bulldog of a man who loved gambling and fine horses. He inspired his workers so that even though they organized a union to challenge his management, they also funded his statue. Witty and generous, Daly brushed off adulation, refused to allow anything to be named for him, and rejected all attempts to recruit him as a candidate for public office. "I know my limitations," he once said. But Daly hid in plain sight: publicly a man of the people, he trusted few and played a long game. The record shows he was adept at keeping his plans hidden until it was time to strike.[274]

Clark, in contrast, was described as a "wire-haired terrier." He was fastidious and formally educated, refined in manner with cultural pretensions. He was vain, openly ambitious, and quick to act. Clark was respected though not well-liked. He was often an open book. He wrote voluminously and shared his opinions even when silence may have been wiser. While Clark enjoyed the spotlight, he may have trusted no one at all. Yet Samuel Hauser noticed Clark valued one thing more than money: "the flattery and admiration of his fellow man."[275]

David Emmons proposed the theory that Daly and Clark's rivalry stemmed from the centuries-old conflict between "the orange and the green," as each man had roots in Ulster. That certainly could have been a factor: Presbyterians such as Clark's ancestors faced discrimination from the rulers of Britain, fleeing prejudice and poverty from Scotland to Ireland. Meanwhile, Daly, an Irish Catholic, viewed these same people as English collaborators and oppressors.[276]

Nonetheless, they both knew how to keep their powder dry. Howard noted the men maintained a "surface semblance of cordiality." In 1900, when the Clark-Daly feud reached the United States Senate, Clark acknowledged the two had always been polite to one another face to face. They could not avoid crossing paths in both their business and personal lives. Clark's brother, J. Ross, married Margaret Daly's sister Miriam "Myra" Evans in April 1878. In the years that followed, extended family gatherings must have become increasingly interesting.[277]

"Anchoring"

As 1877 began, Butte ran four stamp mills, two arastras, and Olin's concentrator. But "the hope and anxiety of the camp [was] the Rainbow lode." Reports from the Alice announced a thirty-foot-wide silver vein was uncovered at ninety-five feet. County records show Daly bought Butcher's shares in the Rising Star lode in February, and then, perhaps imitating the Walkers' real estate investments in Alta, Daly purchased several residential lots in Butte.[278]

Daly "anchored" in Montana when he moved Margaret and the girls in March. Maggie was three years old; Molly was barely one. They settled in a house at the base of the Alice hill. "A good sign, that," declared the *New North-West*. Daly's extended family trickled into Montana. Zenas Evans moved his household to Butte and opened a lumber yard. Margaret Daly's sister Jane arrived with her husband, James Shields, another former Utah mine superintendent. The O'Farrells and Daly's brother Patrick arrived in the 1880s.[279]

In the spring of 1877, Rob Walker brought up the Ophir Stamp Mill as promised, along with an experienced mill operator, Lathrop Dunn. Everyone set to work, Daly below ground directing work on the rich vein of silver ore mixed with gold, while Walker and Dunn set up the mill and expanded it to run twenty stamps. A whim was hoisting ore by April 17. In June, the Alice shaft reached one hundred feet. They began pumping water from ever-deeper shafts, using the runoff to power machinery. The operation economized on freight, as the Walkers' own line handled shipping. The Alice's first silver left Butte on November 7, 1877. By December, the works had grossed $40,000.[280]

Meanwhile, Clark slowly began developing the Moulton, nestled next door to the Alice. His list of sins no doubt lengthened in Daly's eyes as Clark saved the cost of pumping groundwater by waiting to deepen his shaft until groundwater flowed into the Alice sump, forcing Daly and the Walkers to bear the work and expense of draining both properties.[281]

Workers and speculators poured into town. By May 1877, Rolla Butcher ran a large boardinghouse near the Alice that became known as the Rainbow House, and a neighborhood in the vicinity is still called Butchertown. But the community that grew up on the steep slopes around the Alice Works was not named Butchertown for Rolla—or Rainbow after the lode. It became Walkerville.[282]

The Big Hole

Western Montana panicked in June 1877, when a group of nontreaty Nez Perce (Nimiipuu), pursued by the U.S. military, began a 1,100-mile journey from their homeland in eastern Washington Territory. They avoided Fort Missoula and a hastily built redoubt later nicknamed "Fort Fizzle." Then they traveled peacefully south through the Bitterroot Valley and over the mountains toward the Big Hole River. Montana's territorial Governor Benjamin Potts made a call for armed volunteers. The residents of Butte organized a battalion, and W.A. Clark, declaring, "I am at command," was made a major.[283]

The volunteers were not needed. At 3:30 a.m. on August 9, 1877, Colonel John Gibbon's troops from Fort Shaw launched a sneak attack on the Nez Perce camp in the Big Hole Valley. After a fierce four-day battle, the Nez Perce retreated toward Yellowstone National Park, forced to leave

Chief Joseph's band of the Nez Perce. Lapwai, Idaho, spring 1877. *Northwest Museum of Arts and Culture.*

behind ninety of their dead, many of whom were women and children. Their journey ended that October when their last remaining leader, Chief Joseph, surrendered to Generals Nelson Miles and Oliver Howard, whose troops trapped them in the Bear Paw Mountains, about fifty miles from safe refuge in Canada.[284]

In the wake of the Battle of the Big Hole, Butte's volunteer corps regrouped as an armed escort for horse-drawn ambulances to bring about forty wounded soldiers up to the hospital at Deer Lodge. Daly stepped up to raise money for medical supplies. According to Shoebotham, Daly also drove one of the ambulances, stopping at the Warm Springs Ranch of Morgan Evans, who offered his land as a staging ground for the operation. This may have been how Daly met Evans, who was later a key player in developing the town of Anaconda.[285] This trip to the Big Hole may have been the "relief party" mentioned in the *American Turf.* From the battle site, Daly certainly would have noticed the forested mountains to the west; on the other side of the Continental Divide was the Bitterroot Valley.

UNIONIZATION

Long before Daly hoisted copper from the Anaconda, his boldness and charisma made headlines. In March 1878, Helena's *Independent Record* touted his accomplishments: "To Mr. Daly, Montana, and especially Deer Lodge County, owes much of its present prosperity."[286] Daly's popularity probably grated on Clark, who craved the adulation that Daly received. Even as his brother Ross courted Myra Evans, Clark may have been plotting: another account of the Clark-Daly feud's origin said Clark wrote to the Walkers at some unspecified point, claiming that Daly was mismanaging the Alice. According to the story, the Walkers not only dismissed the missive as unfounded, but they shared it with Daly.[287]

Daly's most public mistake was self-inflicted, and he learned an unforgettable lesson. Although operations were profitable, Daly joined with A.J. Davis at the Lexington to cut miners' wages from $3.50 a day to $3.00. The furious workers—both above and below ground—organized, and the Butte Workingmen's Union (later the Butte Miners' Union) was born on June 13, 1878, setting Butte on the road to becoming "the Gibraltar" of American unionism.[288]

Walkerville, 1878, showing Alice mine and structures. *BSB.*

When 150 men presented their grievances, Daly listened sympathetically but claimed he had to consult with the Walkers. Davis sanctimoniously lectured them. Rebuffed in both cases, the union wasted no time in calling a strike. Perhaps seeing opportunity in stirring the pot, W.A. Clark publicly supported the union's efforts. After a two-month strike, both mines repealed the wage cut, and workers returned. In Butte, Miners' Union Day is still celebrated every June 13 in remembrance.[289]

EXPANDING

By November 1879, the Alice shaft was down to the five-hundred-foot level. Meanwhile, Clark took another run at copper reduction. His experiments in 1872 had been unprofitable, but in 1879, he brought in outside investors and built the Colorado smelter. It processed twelve tons of ore a day, producing a crude matte that was 60 percent copper and also yielded eight hundred ounces of silver per ton.[290]

Daly's management of the Alice did not preclude him from scouting new prospects and making independent investments. Daly teamed up with Charles Larrabee, and the pair bought the copper-bearing St. Lawrence mine from Ed Hickey and Valentine Kropf on June 23, 1877. The recorded consideration for the deal was seventy-five dollars, though, in 1895, Daly cryptically commented, "We invested more than a few hundred dollars in the purchase of the St. Lawrence before we owned it all." They patented the claim in July 1879. Daly and Larrabee also patented the Orphan Girl mine and, farther afield, bonded "quartz property" north of Avon on McClellan and Jefferson Gulches.[291]

Daly prospected for others as well. It is not known when Daly met James Ben Ali Haggin in person, but the *Independent Record* revealed in March 1878 that Daly was scouting mines for Haggin in the Helena area. Samuel Hauser mentioned it in his correspondence with A.J. Davis, stating "[Daly] represents Hagin [*sic*] in all matters." K. Ross Toole hypothesized that Daly also told Haggin of a Butte prospect. Next to the St. Lawrence was a claim owned by Ed Hickey's brother, Michael—the Anaconda.[292]

Nonetheless, Daly focused mostly on the Alice, which, by 1880, was producing $1.3 million annually. A sixty-stamp mill augmented the twenty stamps that were already operating. The Alice used the Reese River process of pan amalgamation, a modification of the Washoe process that extracted lead sulfide in galena and other complex silver ores.[293]

The Walkers brought Clayton back to assess the Alice in January 1880 and then took the company public in February, selling $10 million worth of stock at $25 a share, making it the first mining company in Butte listed on the New York Stock Exchange. Ultimately, the Walkers made more money from the Alice than from any of their Utah mining ventures.[294]

THE "WEST SIDE"

This part of the country is getting "horse" on the brain almost as bad as Kentucky.[295]

Daly happily embraced Butte's social life. He nurtured his Irishness in the evenings, visiting his neighbor Ben Stack and reading from the *Irish World*. He helped organize a St. Patrick's Day dance in March 1877, right after moving Margaret and the children.[296]

He also lent a hand to the community. In October 1879, he helped organize a fundraiser to pay off the debt of the Walkerville School, where Rolla Butcher's daughter Emma was the teacher. Daly's involvement makes sense; his daughter Maggie was six years old. Daly was not especially public in matters of faith, but Butte's first Catholic Church, St. Patrick's, also completed its parish building that year. It is likely that Daly contributed to the construction fund.[297]

When networking and fun moved outdoors, horse racing was Daly's—and Montana's—sport of choice. There was little news of horse racing in the Summit Valley before 1877, but Butte's racers competed at Olin's course in Deer Lodge and other tracks. As roads improved, Sunday afternoons in Butte presented opportunities for speed trials on the flats. Just as fast men trotted from tavern to tavern in New York, Butte had drinking establishments strategically located at precisely measured intervals, such as the "Three-Mile."[298]

As elsewhere, the growing town soon frowned upon informal contests as both a physical and a moral hazard to the respectable crowd. The speedsters had to find a new venue.

A direct connection between Daly reaching Butte and the development of the city's racetrack is unlikely, as Montana already had "horse on the brain" and organized tracks from Missoula to Bozeman. But Daly no doubt applauded the news on June 12, 1877, that William Owsley was staking out a racecourse. Owsley was a livery stable owner and the county road supervisor. He helped build the road from Butte to Helena and had the equipment, workhorses, and expertise to handle the project.[299]

William Owsley. *BSB.*

Owsley's livery partner was Henry G. Valiton. Valiton leased the track, formed a committee, and set up Butte's first meet in 1878. The West Side Racing Meeting sent off trotters and runners on October 9 for five freezing cold days of racing. The "West Side" name has confused historians, as the track was on the flats east of town (East Middle School and the Racetrack neighborhood now occupy the site). The name probably referred to Butte being on the west side of the Continental Divide, contrasted with Bozeman's Eastern Montana Racing Association east of the divide. The weather kept spectators to about two hundred a day but led to greater things. Butte ultimately ran sixty-day race meets with crowds in the thousands.[300]

The power brokers now had the perfect place to congregate, and the "committee" that organized the meet was another example of the role horse racing played in the political, business, and social world of the 1800s. It is not a coincidence that Owsley and Valiton each later served as the mayor of Butte.[301]

Another committee stalwart was a friend and neighbor of Daly's, John Noyes (1829–1902). A Canadian who reached Butte in 1866, Noyes invested in waterworks. He was a partner with Daly on some mining claims, served in the territorial legislature, and retired as another of Butte's millionaires.[302]

Most notably, the committee nurtured Lee Mantle (1851–1934). The young Englishman reached Butte in 1877 as a telegrapher at the Wells Fargo office. He soon moved into insurance and real estate and then partnered in Owsley and Valiton's livery business. Later, Mantle obtained title to the land under the racetrack. He established the *Daily Inter-Mountain* newspaper in 1881, the same year he became the racing secretary of the West Side meet. He represented Butte as a territorial legislator, followed Owsley and Valiton as mayor of Butte, and ultimately, Montana voters sent Mantle to the United States Senate in 1895.[303]

Lee Mantle. *Wikimedia Commons.*

Both Clark and Daly appear on the West Side Racing Association's articles of incorporation from 1886. But Daly, though not a founding member, joined the committee well before Clark. When the committee organized a meet on the Fourth of July 1879, the *Miner* commented on June 10, "Mr. Marcus Daly of Walkerville and John McCormick of Butte have been added to the committee to canvass Butte and Walkerville for funds for our Fourth of July celebration." Daly's involvement correlates with his first visible embrace of political power. He was a Democratic Party delegate to the territorial convention in July 1879.[304]

Daly may have done more fundraising behind the scenes. When Butte's fall meet opened in September 1879, the grounds were much improved, boasting a covered grandstand, a restaurant, and a bar. The committee, now officially the West Side Racing Association, welcomed another politician: Montana's territorial governor Benjamin F. Potts, who arrived with his own racing string. Extending an olive branch to the miners, no doubt bowing to the inevitability that many would skip their shift anyway, the Lexington shut down for a day to "give the boys a chance to see the horse races, also to stake their money on the Walkerville fleet-foot, who walked away with the race, as was expected." It is not known if Daly offered this deal at the Alice, but he later gave time off—with pay—on opening day as a benefit to his workers at the Anaconda Company.[305]

The growth of Butte's racetrack provided a surface hint that bigger things were happening underground. Nationally, a copper boom was looming. In Menlo Park, New Jersey, on December 31, 1879, Thomas Edison rang in the new year of 1880 by publicly demonstrating his newest invention: the incandescent light bulb.

THE ANACONDA

In 1866, Michael Hickey (1836–1909) wandered the Butte Hill. In an interview thirty years later, he claimed he saw "copper carbonate" laying around on the ground in green chunks the size of walnuts.* But seeking gold, not copper, he did not bother to file a claim. By 1875, Hickey was interested in silver and teamed up with his younger brother Ed (1841–1921). They established themselves on the Butte Hill with neighboring claims.[306]

Ed named his claim the St. Lawrence for the New York county where the Hickeys grew up. Michael sought a more unique name. He was a Civil War veteran and was inspired by Horace Greeley's characterization of Union forces surrounding the Confederates "like a giant anaconda." On October 19, 1875, he went to the courthouse in Deer Lodge and named his claim the Anaconda lode, describing it as a silver-bearing property. It was a most prophetic name for the mine that grew into "the Company" that, like the constrictor, came to encompass all of Butte, dominating the economy and politics of Montana for a century.[307]

"Representing"

To hold his claim, Hickey dug an unstable, untimbered hole thirty-five feet deep. He found "free-milling" silver in impressive quantities, and A.J. Davis offered $700 to buy in. However, Hickey wanted labor more than capital.

---

* Copper oxides can be greenish at the surface, but only a few of Butte's outcrops were that color. "Carbonate copper" outcrops tended to be dark red or brown.

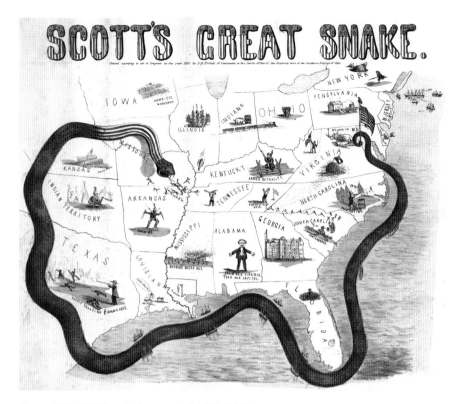

General Winfield Scott's "Anaconda," 1861. *LOC.*

He turned down Davis and partnered with Charles Larrabee, allegedly "for nothing," to help with the work.

Hickey's next problem was W.A. Clark. According to Hickey's 1895 interview, hoisting out silver was barely worth the effort, because Clark charged forty-five dollars a ton to process ore at the Dexter Mill. To streamline operations, Daly came to Hickey's rescue at an unidentified date, offering his expertise to sink the shaft another fifty feet in exchange for a one-third interest.

Daly later claimed he knew from the outset that the Anaconda contained copper. However, though the promising silver lead turned out to be one hundred feet wide, the ore in sight in Michael Hickey's little hole had "not a stain of green."[308]

When Daly started work on the Anaconda, the first thing he did was properly timber Hickey's dangerous shaft. Then, with a hand-cranked windlass, digging recommenced. Daly kept the operation as quiet as possible; his first employees were two he implicitly trusted: his nephew John

O'Farrell Jr. and his "warmly attached companion" Mike Carroll, a fellow Irishman whom he lured away from a job as a shift boss at the Alice. When the operation reached eighty-five feet, Daly offered Hickey a lease, agreed to invest $14,000 in the mine, and bonded a $10,000 option on another one-third interest.[309]

Daly and Hickey controlled the narrative when the *Anaconda Standard* interviewed them in 1895, but their accounts do not entirely align with documentation from 1875 to 1881. For example, Hickey claimed that Daly purchased the St. Lawrence after the Anaconda. Yet county records show Daly and Larrabee purchased at least part of the St. Lawrence in 1877; Daly's interest in the Anaconda was not officially recorded until 1880.[310]

These discrepancies suggest there was a handshake deal before any public record. Officially, on July 10, 1880, Daly and Larrabee purchased a two-thirds undivided interest from Hickey for a consideration of $1,000. Hickey's 1895 recollection was that he sold the entire claim to Daly, but if he did, that deal was under the table, as on October 11, 1880, Daly, Larrabee and Hickey together filed for a patent.[311]

A hand-cranked mining windlass with a bucket, Butte. *BSB.*

An open question is what Daly knew about the Anaconda and when he knew it. The Daly myth claimed he had a mystical ability to "see deeper into the earth than any man"—the same talent attributed to George Hearst. But neither man had need for supernatural skills; they were smart, observant, and learned from the school of hard knocks.

Observation was key. Daly liked to conceal what he was up to until a time of his choosing, but he also gathered intelligence on everyone else. It took effort to keep secrets in early Butte. Reporters prowled the diggings and saloons. Legal notices, courthouse property transfers, and the juiciest gossip were all published in the *Butte Miner*. W.A. Clark eventually bought the paper outright in 1889, making it his personal mouthpiece, while Daly started the *Anaconda Standard* as a foil. But originally, the *Miner* was a simpler publication—the town tabloid with feelers everywhere.

In 1878, the *Miner* was purchased by a group that included Daly, Clark, and Noyes. If the purchase was an attempt to control the flow of news, it was a futile effort. If the *Miner* killed a story, the *New North-West* in Deer Lodge or one of the Helena newspapers were eager for a scoop. But if the goal was to create news or get wind of what was happening before it hit print, Daly had a connection: William Read, the bookkeeper at the Alice who followed Daly to the Anaconda. His brother John B. Read was a reporter at the *Miner*.[312]

Daly also observed mines directly. Shareholders had an inside track, and Silver Bow County property records show Daly bought and sold lode claims at a rate resembling bored miners swapping poker chips back in the gold camps of California.

Daly later claimed he always knew the future of Butte was in copper, which smacks of puffery. That said, he did keep an eye on Charles Meader. Meader was said to know "more about copper ore than any man in the west." He ran Butte's East and West Colusa mines and built the Bell smelter, completed in 1881. The community that sprung up nearby was named Meaderville.[313]

Along with observation and skill, there was an element of luck in mining, but Daly was a gambler who knew how to assess the odds. At the Alice, he saw copper in the waste ore. He patented the St. Lawrence in 1879 as a copper property. When Daly took the plunge and put his name on the Anaconda in 1880, he bet on good odds. Whatever Daly saw gave him confidence to charge full speed ahead.

HUNTING CAPITAL

As promising as the Anaconda silver lead was, Daly needed investors. He notified the Walkers and offered them a chance to buy in. They had an outside expert take a look. It was probably Clayton who visited Butte in January 1880 to assess the Alice. The expert declared, correctly enough, that the Anaconda was not a silver property for the long haul, and the Walkers declined Daly's offer.[314]

Passing on the Anaconda was the Walkers' second financial misstep involving Daly. While they had to know about Butte's copper reserves, they were cautious by nature, and copper presented new challenges they did not need—at the time, they were busy taking the Alice public.

After the Walkers launched the Alice's public offering, a complicated series of transactions followed. Daly sold his interests in the Alice mine and mill to Rob Walker in a multitude of small exchanges. Recorded consideration was at least $30,000, but Daly possibly got as much as $100,000 ($2.4 million in 2020 dollars). He only said, "I made a good sale." Rob then transferred the Walkers' shares to the restructured Alice Gold and Silver Mining Company and filed incorporation in Utah on May 16, 1880.[315]

Newspapers declared the Alice the "Comstock of Montana" and Daly "the ablest mining superintendent," but the relationship between Daly and the Walkers had cooled. Daly's springtime transactions seemed to be clearing title for the corporate entity, but by summer, Daly severed his employment with the Walkers altogether. Salt Lake City newspapers indicated that Daly left the Alice in July 1880, corresponding with Daly's official July 10 purchase of the Anaconda. Rob Walker also transferred some properties to Daly as they consolidated their respective holdings on different parts of the Butte Hill. The "divorce" was complete by September 1880.[316]

By some accounts, Daly broke with the Walkers because he disagreed with their decision to take the Alice public. It is possible. For a minor player like Daly was at the time, the poorly regulated world of nineteenth-century stock trading was a game of smoke and mirrors.[317]

The Walkers later grumbled—mildly—that Daly cheated them on the Anaconda, though their complaint smacked of sour grapes. Daly gave them a chance to buy in; they didn't take it. Daly kept things professional, but in his 1895 interview could not resist a touch of snark: "The money looked large to me, and when I went back to Salt Lake, I thought I would make them respect my bank account anyhow."[318]

There may be a simpler explanation for the break. Daly spent nearly ten years as a manager for the Walkers and perhaps was tired of being second-guessed and overruled. To Daly, the son of an Irish tenant farmer, the Walkers were a family who began with next to nothing and built an empire. He was ready to start on his own.

After the Walkers' snub, Daly next contacted R.C. Chambers, offering him a half-interest in the Anaconda for $10,000. Chambers declined, apparently on account of his own financial limitations at the time. He later explained that he did not want to "put that amount of money into one hole." There were no hard feelings. Daly and Chambers worked together on other enterprises.[319]

It appears that Chambers convinced Daly that he needed the Hearst-Haggin-Tevis syndicate and to visit San Francisco in person to recruit them.[320]

CALIFORNIA NEGOTIATIONS

The *Miner* documented that Daly made three trips from Butte to California in 1880. His first trip was after selling the bulk of his Alice holdings in April. His departure date was not reported, but on May 26, the *Miner* announced his return. Daly publicly used family to justify these California excursions. On the way back, he stopped off in Virginia City, Nevada, where the O'Farrells lived—but so did Daly's mentor John Mackay.[321]

After Daly recorded the Anaconda purchase on July 10, he made a second trip to California. He left on July 26, accompanied by his mother-in-law and her two unmarried daughters. He returned to Butte alone on August 15. On August 17, the *Miner* finally noted Daly's July purchase of the Anaconda but never mentioned he quit the Alice—perhaps it was useful to co-own the local paper.[322]

Connolly, as well as Daly's private secretary John Lindsay (later a district court judge), each recounted a story alleging Daly quit the Alice before he bought the Anaconda, claiming he would take his windfall and move to Grass Valley, California. Although the Daly family visited California in 1880 and a Salt Lake newspaper called him a San Francisco resident in 1881, it is doubtful Daly had any intention of moving. More likely, it was misdirection. Daly was not the only Anaconda partner to leave town claiming personal motives; in the spring of 1880, Charles Larrabee went to Kentucky on a horse-buying expedition.[323]

Margaret and Marcus Daly (undated). *Daly Mansion.*

The Daly legend maintains that Margaret Daly was unhappy about the situation and dropped in on her neighbor John Noyes's wife, Elmira, to whom she lamented her husband's insane decision to quit his job at the Alice. Then, convinced that ruin was just around the corner, Margaret allegedly began taking in laundry to be sure she could pay the family bills.[324] The story is yet to be verified in 1880 sources, but if true, Margaret possibly played a role in Daly's plot of misdirection. Or given the separate spheres in which nineteenth-century husbands and wives moved, it is equally possible that she was out of the loop and truly panicked. In either case, a modern social media thread moves slower than the speed at which Margaret and Elmira's conversation would have become town gossip.

On December 4, 1880, Daly headed west a third time, allegedly "for several months to visit his family." It is unclear when Margaret Daly joined her mother and sisters in the temporary family exodus to the coast. Margaret, Maggie, and Molly were in Butte in June, as recorded by the 1880 census taker. But they were in California in December, as Daly was in San Francisco over Christmas, and it was unlikely Margaret remained in Walkerville doing other people's laundry.[325]

Daly's journeys, one during a Montana winter, are especially remarkable when considering that anyone leaving Butte in 1880 began the trip with a fifteen-hour stagecoach ride to the Utah and Northern Railroad terminus at Red Rock, roughly one hundred miles to the south. After another twenty-four hours, if all went well without derailments, track washouts, or other unscheduled delays, passengers reached Ogden, Utah, where they transferred to the transcontinental rails for a forty-two-hour ride to San Francisco.[326]

On January 18, 1881, Daly was back in Butte, along with John O'Farrell Jr., both having allegedly returned from "a pleasure trip to the Bay." Daly's decision to bring O'Farrell with him on his winter trip was notable. Not only had his nephew been working in the Anaconda, he was one of Daly's closest confidantes, a protégé, and perhaps an heir apparent. When O'Farrell died of typhoid in 1888, a devastated Daly said, "I have lost a real friend, one of the few who understood me and my ways."[327]

Clearly, Daly's trips were not merely a "pleasure trip to the bay." That said, Daly sending his family to California and claiming he would move there kept the town gossips—and his competition—unaware of what he was up to.

The Hearst-Haggin-Tevis Syndicate was expanding. In 1877, Hearst bought the Homestake gold mine in Lead, South Dakota. By 1878, he was called the "Black Hills Bonanza King," and the syndicate took the Homestake Mining Company public in 1879. In 1880, Hearst reactivated his political career and purchased a newspaper, the *San Francisco Daily Examiner*, which he turned over to his son seven years later, initiating William Randolph Hearst's journalism empire. Hearst also owed a favor to Daly. By 1881, Utah's Ontario was the leading silver mine in the nation; the Walkers' properties ranked eighth.[328]

Wells Fargo and Company was the tip of Haggin and Tevis's iceberg. Their investments included not only Rancho del Paso but also a massive irrigation project that turned 400,000 acres they owned in Kern County, California, into the agricultural heart of the state. They ultimately controlled 1.5 million acres. When Haggin and Tevis restructured their partnership in January 1881, the newspapers explained, "Their business has assumed such gigantic proportions…that they were unable to manage it."[329]

According to Lindsay, as Daly negotiated in California, he kept in touch with Butte via coded telegrams. The code that indicated the ore showed promise was "cattle doing well on the hill." Disappointing results were conveyed by saying, "Cattle doing poorly in the valley." Throughout this time, the Anaconda was "vigorously developed," revealing a significant amount of "free ore"—silver.[330] Overall, the cattle did well on the hill.

THE PARTNERSHIP

Later accounts claimed Daly fooled everyone by acting as if silver was playing out in the Anaconda so he could snap up neighboring claims cheaply. It is questionable if he fooled knowledgeable miners, though Daly drew attention away from the Anaconda. In March 1881, he contracted to sink a three-hundred-foot shaft at the Original. In April, he partnered in the North Star and the Salisbury mines north of Walkerville. On May 3, he formed the Stevens Gold and Silver Mining Company.[331]

His biggest plans were successfully kept under wraps until May 31, 1881, when the *Miner* finally revealed the California game, stating, "Marcus Daly lately sold the Anaconda mine to parties living on the Pacific coast." The transaction was recorded on June 2, 1881, listing Haggin as agent. Consideration was $30,000, but Daly probably received $100,000 in total.[332]

According to the research of Michael Malone, Hearst held 39 percent of the new Anaconda Gold and Silver Mining Company; Haggin, 26 percent; Daly, 25 percent; and Tevis, 10 percent. It was interesting that Haggin, not Hearst, put his name as agent for the transaction. Perhaps it was one of Haggin's strategic gambles. By at least one account, when Hearst presented Daly's proposal to the syndicate, Haggin recommended it be a partnership with Daly.[333]

Behind the scenes, the deal was complicated. County records filed on May 28, 1881, just a few days before Daly transferred the Anaconda to Haggin, show that Larrabee and Hickey sold a two-thirds interest in the Anaconda to Daly for consideration of $20,000. But what is intriguing is that the contract to sell was made on September 1, 1880, *prior* to their application for a patent that October. Keeping the transfer under wraps for nine months as the deal incubated was impressive—and Daly's style, misdirection and hiding in plain sight while waiting for the right moment to strike.[334]

Having loyal colleagues helped. Long before Daly started the *Anaconda Standard*, he nurtured friendships with journalists. For example, on a return trip from San Francisco in July 1881, he stopped over in Salt Lake City. There, he confided in another longtime acquaintance, C.C. Goodwin, the editor of the *Salt Lake Tribune*. The two may have met back in White Pine, Nevada, where Goodwin edited the local paper. Goodwin recalled in 1912, "[Daly] said to me then [in 1881] that the world did not know it, but it would after a while, that he had the biggest mine ever found."[335]

The Daly family re-anchored in Butte. In April, Daly began building a house at the intersection of Montana and Quartz Streets, a plot occupied today by the Butte-Silver Bow Courthouse Complex. Amid the frenzy, Margaret, Maggie, and Molly returned from the coast, though their return date was not documented. Construction was finished in September, the family moved in, and Margaret formally received callers on January 2, 1882.[336]

Hearst came to town to see the Anaconda's operation firsthand. It is unclear when he arrived; on July 3, 1881, he had mail waiting in Butte at general delivery. R.C. Chambers visited on July 27. Hearst's presence in Montana was not confirmed until September 3, when Helena's *Independent Record* scooped the Butte newspapers. The absence of local news suggests Daly tried to keep Hearst's visit quiet.[337]

Later tales allege Hearst told Daly where to sink a new shaft, but Daly had started on an 8x20 three-compartment design in June. Hearst did approve a plan for the mine to make crosscuts every one hundred feet, drifting east and west for three hundred to five hundred feet. In November 1881, equipment reached Butte capable of sinking a shaft one thousand feet. As expected, there was rich silver ore mixed with some copper. Hearst and Daly decided to process the Anaconda's free-milling silver at W.A. Clark's ten-stamp Dexter mill, and Daly closed a one-year lease with Clark to begin July 2, 1882.[338]

"Getting Wood for Colorado Smelter," Butte area. *BSB.*

This might have been when Hearst and Daly visited the Bitterroot area, scouting timber. They needed a steady supply. The nature of Butte's deposits meant that the unstable walls of the stopes and tunnels required innovative square-set framing with massive timbers, and the timber-rich slopes north of Butte at Elk Park were being stripped bare. Daly wound up making timber investments in western Montana with partners such as Missoula's A.B. Hammond before starting his own lumber mill in Hamilton in 1891.[339]

As Daly worked silver in 1881 with a respectable bank account and the support of America's most successful mining syndicate, he certainly knew copper lurked below. He had transitioned from gold in California to silver in Nevada. His next set of challenges was how to mine Montana copper and make it pay.

DAWN OF A COPPER EMPIRE

It seemed though the sun had suddenly arisen,
such was the intensity of the light.[340]

Butte's vast copper deposits needed three things: a market, transportation, and reduction capacity.

Early experiments revealed that copper carried an electric current better than any other nonprecious metal. Demand for copper came from an ever-increasing market for electricity. Nineteenth-century inventions such as the electromagnet and the telegraph modestly increased demand, but then Bell's telephone and Edison's light bulb captured the imagination of America. By 1880, the copper market was poised to expand exponentially.

The Wild West embraced new technology as eagerly as the rest of the world. Butte soon installed its first brush dynamo to generate electricity, and on a snowy night in November 1880, people gazed toward Walkerville as Montana's first dozen electric arc lights blazed in the sky, illuminating the hoisting works of the Alice.[341]

The copper wire that turned the Alice's night into day arrived after a complex process and a journey of many thousands of miles. Wire had to be over 99 percent pure copper to properly conduct current. For Butte's own copper to do the job, the crude ore from the mines went halfway around the world and back.[342] It would not pay off until shipping and reduction costs stopped eating the profits.

THE BATHOLITH

Everyone knew the Butte Hill contained copper. As early as November 1867, miners griped about it, considering it a nuisance. In the silver-rich mines of Walkerville's Rainbow lode, it was a waste product. Yet when Billy Parks hit the Parrott's rich copper glace, and when the Anaconda's diggings found chalcocite at three hundred feet, it was obvious that copper was abundant enough to be worth mining.

The first challenge was geology. By 1961, when the Anaconda Company's Mountain Consolidated mine reached 5,280 feet, Butte was truly "mile high, mile deep." But even the Mountain Con merely scratched the massive geologic formation beneath the hill. The Boulder Batholith runs from Butte to just south of Helena—an area sixty by thirty-five miles—and plunges over seven miles into the Earth's crust.

Geography of the Boulder Batholith. *Richard I. Gibson.*

The Batholith did not give up its riches easily. Formed during the Cretaceous epoch seventy to eighty million years ago, its magma cooled unevenly. Molten solutions solidified into veins that twisted crazily through coarse-grained granite and fine porphyry. Varying temperatures and pressures created many different minerals.

Early miners described mineralization that outcropped on the surface in green bands. Deep underground, copper ores included the sulfides: bornite, chalcocite, colusite, covellite, digenite, and enargite. Carbonates and oxides occurred nearer the surface; blue azurite, red cuprite, and green malachite winked seductively from veins altered by water and oxygen.[343]

Profits came from purity. The term *refractory* describes ore that is difficult to reduce to bullion, and Butte's chemically complex copper ore was notoriously refractory. Sulfur had to be removed, often along with arsenic and other undesirable elements. Samples were touted as 80 percent copper, but the ore also held widely varying amounts of silver with a trace of gold. Useful but mundane elements such as iron, lead, manganese, molybdenum, and zinc were also in the mix.[344] The trick was separating it.

REDUCING ORE

Michigan copper dominated the industry. The Keweenaw Peninsula, jutting into Lake Superior, held easily refined native copper from the purest deposits on Earth, some first worked by Native people over seven thousand years ago. Michigan's smelters used relatively simple technology to refine their free-milling ore.[345]

Giles Olin's Cornish jig used a process similar to Michigan's to crush ore, adding water to separate gangue. But unlike the Keweenaw's copper, Butte's refractory copper wasn't quietly waiting to be extracted from crushed-up rock with heat and a few chemicals to coax out minor impurities. It was sterner stuff, far beyond Montana's technology in the 1870s. The only thing early miners could do then was feed separated ore into primitive smelting furnaces, melting it into a crude matte before shipping it elsewhere.

The capacity of outside facilities presented more barriers. Michigan's copper interests were unwilling to help the competition, and their refineries could not handle complex ore anyway. Some Montana copper was shipped

Left: Chalcocite from the Anaconda mine, 1883. *Daniel Evanich.*

Right: Complex ore containing chalcocite, enargite, pyrite, and digenite, Steward Mine. *Daniel Evanich.*

to Colorado and Baltimore, but these small facilities could not handle large volumes nor extract arsenic from Butte's most refractory ore. Thus, much of Butte's copper went overseas to Swansea, Wales—only the copper refining capital of the world could do it all.[346]

The distances involved meant shipped ore had to average over 30 percent copper just to break even. When Parks and Ramsdell tried smelting copper ore back in 1866, they lacked the ability to flux it to a profitable purity. When Ramsdell teamed up with Charles Hendrie in 1868, they produced only modestly better results before that project also failed.[347]

Hendrie did send Butte's first shipment of copper to Swansea in July 1868. He hauled a ton and a half of "pigs"—ingots of crudely smelted ore—to Fort Benton and loaded them onto the steamboat *Mountaineer*. It cost forty dollars a ton to get ore to St. Louis. Then for another ten dollars a ton, it went down the Mississippi River to New Orleans. After that, doubling as ballast, Montana copper crossed the Atlantic to Swansea. Hendrie's "pigs" ranged from 25 percent to 71 percent copper, but it was the silver and gold they also contained that made the enterprise profitable.[348]

Even W.A. Clark failed to return a dollar with another stuck to it when he shipped ore running 35 percent pure to Baltimore in 1872. Ultimately, many of Butte's mines resorted to open heap roasting, creating layered stacks of copper ore and firewood, some covering up to an acre of land. The wood ignited the sulphides, which would then burn for weeks on end, oxidizing the sulfur and arsenic into the atmosphere, and reducing the copper to a crumbling "calcine" that could be smelted into a 60 percent matte. Meader's

Bell smelter was an early adopter of the process, lighting up the first stacks in 1880, and as stinking yellow smoke billowed into the sky, it was—at least at first—hard to argue with success.[349]

But without better and cheaper transportation, copper from the Butte Hill languished on the ore dumps.

The Utah and Northern

In 1880, Butte's population reached three thousand, and on February 16, 1881, the legislature carved Silver Bow County from Deer Lodge County, making Butte the county seat. No longer would miners trek forty miles to record mining claims and property transfers. But Deer Lodge was losing commerce and a lucrative tax base, so the event created significant drama in the territorial legislature. Desperate vandals even cut the telegraph line between Butte and Deer Lodge in a futile attempt to stop the plan from going through. But in the end, Deer Lodge congratulated the new county, wryly calling it "a rib from our side" and the "Silver Queen of the West."[350]

The victory revealed the political power of the West Side Racing Association. Several past and future members were on Silver Bow County's governing committee, including Butte's new mayor Henry Valiton, Marcus Daly, Lee Mantle, and John Noyes.[351]

But "Silver Queen" status notwithstanding, railroads had to reach Butte before anyone would put serious money into a copper operation.

Throughout the 1870s, Fort Benton's steamboats handled the most profitable freight: outbound gold and inbound finished goods. Silver went south, as the Montana Trail was longer but cheaper. Freight wagons trudged to the Utah railheads at three miles per hour. Some large teams of up to twenty animals pulled three wagons coupled together. These train-like contraptions averaged fifteen miles a day. Montana winters allowed travel between only April and November. Food, tools, and equipment filled the wagons returning to Montana. But the volume of copper ore needing transport required cheaper rates than freight wagons could offer, yet without a promise of large ore shipments to pick up, railroads had little interest in expanding north. Neither railroads nor mines would invest without guarantees from the other.[352]

The Mormon Church tried to break the stalemate. Utah farmers saw Montana as a promising market for agricultural produce, and the Latter-day Saints saw potential for expanded settlement. With limited funds, they formed the Utah Northern, a narrow-gauge railway, in 1872. By 1874, the project connected Logan to the Union Pacific. But going farther north presented engineering challenges, plus the railroad ran out of funds. The rails stalled just over the Utah border in Franklin, Idaho, not far from the Boa Ogoi site.[353]

As the Alice and other Montana mines sent out ever-larger shipments of silver, the railroad interests finally looked at expanding north. In 1878, the Utah Northern project gained a new lease on life when financier Jay Gould and the Union Pacific took over. Renamed the Utah and Northern Railroad, construction resumed. Initially, Helena was the proposed terminus for the line, but as it progressed, Butte became the target. Ultimately, the 466-mile-long line connected to the Northern Pacific at Garrison.[354]

None of this was a mystery to Marcus Daly, who mastered the art of having tentacles in many directions. In 1879, his father-in-law, Zenas Evans, was part-owner of a sawmill in the Snake River Valley of Idaho. Evans obtained a railroad contract for 750,000 board feet of timber and 40,000 railroad ties. The contract said the sawmill would move north with the terminus of the railroad.[355] There was no better source of intelligence.

The press avidly followed the rails' progress. On March 9, 1880, the "silver spike" was driven in at Monida Pass on the Montana-Idaho line, and the *Miner* erupted with a word salad of glee, congratulating "thou mighty stalwart of the wonderful northland."[356]

Day by day, the *Miner* and the *New North-West* lovingly described every inch of track laid to the next "terminus"—which became the town of Dillon—where building paused in the winter of 1880. In June 1881, the newspapers' breathless prose resumed as the railroad headed for the Silver Bow County line and reached the brand-new town of Melrose. By November 2, the tracks reached Silver Bow Junction (near the present-day I-90/I-15 interchange near Rocker). Finally, on December 21, 1881, at 11:10 p.m., the first official train from Ogden, Utah, arrived in Butte.[357]

For copper, the timing was perfect.

THE CHECKBOOK

At Daly's statue unveiling in 1907, endless flowery speeches from politicians and Amalgamated Copper Company officials were reprinted in column

Butte, 1882. *BSB.*

after column of the next day's newspapers. But one stands out: Con Kelley's tale of when copper was discovered in the Anaconda:

> *There is standing in this throng today a man now grown into the silver tinge of age, who told me long ago the story of how ore was first struck in the mighty Anaconda. Down in the darkness, lighted only by the candles flickering ray, day after day, with unremitting toil, the crosscut had steadily been advanced, when one day the drills encountered a new material.... Behind the workmen stood Mr. Daly and his lieutenant, bluff, kind-hearted old Mike Carroll....Holes were loaded, the fuse ignited, the blast exploded; with hurrying steps and palpitating hearts they hastened to the breast of the drift. Mr. Daly picked up a mass of glistening rock, and impulsively exclaimed: "Mike, we've got it!"* [358]

Again, what did Daly know about the Anaconda—and when was it common knowledge? Kelley's story notwithstanding, the big copper strike may have been next door. On January 27, 1882, the *Miner* noted, "A fine ore body has been struck in the St. Lawrence."[359]

In February, Daly made a short trip to Salt Lake City and boasted of Butte to the press, which reported, "[Daly] declares Butte...never was half as full of promise as at present." By May 1882, there were plenty of rumors about the future of Butte copper but few mysteries as to direction. Both the Anaconda and the St. Lawrence were mentioned in a longer list of mines containing copper and producing well. On June 1, 1882, the *Miner* declared Butte a "copper camp," boasting, "the copper wealth of Butte is far more vast than even its own citizens suppose."[360]

The papers bemoaned a lack of reduction capacity. The Montana, Bell, Parrot, and Colorado had small copper smelters but could barely handle output from their own mines, processing a combined fifty tons of ore per day. Butte shipped silver bullion produced by the Reese River process, but the best copper they could deliver was "matte": partially reduced ore, far from pure. Nonetheless, by the spring of 1882, copper from the St. Lawrence shipped to Baltimore. Still waiting on the dump was one hundred tons of ore claimed to run 40 to 45 percent copper—along with four hundred tons of "lower-grade" ore.[361]

To outward appearances, the Anaconda remained focused on silver. On June 11, the *Miner* noted $200,000 was sunk into the project yet made an odd claim that "not a pound of pay ore has ever been shipped from this property." The reporter also noticed that quietly sitting on the Anaconda dump was twenty tons of ore claimed to run 44 percent copper, concluding in the piece that the Anaconda might be about to pay off: "They are now rewarded with immense ore reserves which will take a long time to exhaust."[362]

It was no secret something big was in the works. On June 9, 1882, Daly left town, and the *Miner* had a scoop: "The Anaconda stockholders will have a meeting in San Francisco in a few days." Rail travel made the trip to the coast less daunting; the Butte to Ogden leg was cut down to twenty-six hours. Even with layovers and transfers, Daly was presumably in San Francisco by about June 13.[363] On June 24, Daly either returned or at least sent a telegram with good news, as the *Miner* trumpeted:

> *The next great mining enterprise will doubtless be the erection in Butte by the Anaconda Copper and Silver Mining Company of the largest smelting plant on the Pacific Coast* [sic]. *It is thought this was definitely resolved on at the recent meeting of stockholders in San Francisco. Certain it is that the Anaconda mine is well deserving of such enterprise.*[364]

Behind the scenes, a miracle occurred.

Daly's trip to California was ill-timed. Hearst was in the heat of a campaign, seeking the Democratic nomination for governor of

California. He arranged laudatory editorials in his own newspaper and lavishly distributed funds to convention delegates. It was all for naught; after fourteen ballots, on June 23, 1882, the convention nominated George Stoneman. Tevis was also distracted, focused on California business matters and the appointment of railroad commissioners.[365]

Daly's meeting occurred amid this whirlwind. Probably taking the most upbeat tone he could muster, Daly announced the copper deposits to his partners, presented a plan for a significant expansion of the works at Anaconda, and recommended the development of a smelter. His announcement went over like the proverbial lead balloon.

Hearst expressed concern about new expenses. Between new mining investments in Arizona, California politics, and the *Examiner*, he was probably bleeding money and uninterested in bankrolling anything new. Some accounts say he largely ignored Daly, discussing other business with Tevis.[366]

Tevis was already unhappy about the money sunk into the project. He thought Daly was "chasing a chimera" and suggested an assessment of all four stockholders to fund the expansion. Daly protested, saying he could not afford it. Tevis then declared that Daly's only alternative was to sell out. Though some accounts attribute this attempted "freezeout" to Hearst, the behavior was classic Tevis, who was abrupt, tight-fisted, and controlling; in earlier years, he even tried and failed to control Phoebe Hearst's pocketbook when Hearst was off on business.[367]

Haggin quietly observed the exchange. Perhaps Haggin saw in the Irishman a kindred spirit who shoved aside ethnic slurs and prejudice to carve a successful path in the world. Maybe he recognized a fellow plunger who knew how to calculate the odds. In any case, Haggin made a dramatic move.

He took out a checkbook. Signing every blank check it contained, Haggin handed it to Daly. The dialogue may have been invented or embellished by later writers, but Haggin reminded Tevis that if Daly was broke, he was not, and declared, "I'll see Daly through on this deal." To Daly, he allegedly said, "Take that checkbook and pay your assessments with it as long as I have a dollar in the bank. When you need more, draw and keep drawing."[368]

Daly dashed back to Montana, and by August 1882, the Anaconda mine was a hive of workers. Daly installed a larger, powerful new hoisting engine. His goal was speed; the 1872 Mining Law allowed Daly to follow a vein as far as it went, but Butte's copper belt of fractured veins was estimated to be three miles long and a half-mile wide. Other mines were digging into the same deposits, and possession was nine-tenths of the law.[369]

The significance of Haggin's act is memorialized in 10,607 feet of stone. The mountain peak south of what became Daly's new town of Anaconda was named Mount Haggin.* John Lindsay claimed Haggin was the only person who ever inspired awe in Daly, but Haggin was also a friend. Along with Mackay, Rogers, and Scallon, Haggin was one of the eight pallbearers at Daly's funeral.[370]

For Daly personally, the biggest event of 1882 occurred at home. Margaret delivered their third child, Marcus Daly II, on August 14. It had been six years since Molly's birth in 1876. A new house, hired help, and a secure income ushered a new Daly into the world. The Dalys' final child, Harriot, was born in 1884. The future showed promise.

MAKING NOISE

In September 1882, the *Salt Lake Tribune* declared:

> *Among all the mining camps of the coast* [west of the Continental Divide], *in our judgement, Butte, Montana, is to be one of the longest-lived and most steadily prosperous. The ores are hard to mine and to work; it requires heavy capital to place a mining enterprise there on a paying basis, but there is a fair profit in working the ore and there is more ore than any other camp on the coast ever showed. These last two facts insure* [sic] *the permanency of the place. There are already more than 200 stamps dropping steadily in the district: there are three or four extensive copper-reduction works, and these will be increased indefinitely in the future, for the ore is there….By next year, the Anaconda and St. Lawrence and others will begin to make a noise.*[371]

And noise there was. As 1882 edged into 1883, Daly's plans swung into action. He had no way to know that he would not live to see the age of sixty, but he built an empire as if he knew time was short. In November 1882, the *Miner* discreetly noted that Morgan Evans sold property on Upper Warm Springs Creek to the Anaconda Mining Company, "whom it is understood will erect thereon extensive smelting works."[372] Daly broke

---

* A reservoir named "Lake Hearst" was created in 1897. The forty-two-acre body of water is still part of the watershed for the town of Anaconda. There is a smaller "Haggin Lake" in an adjacent drainage. No Montana landforms are named for Tevis, but given how he treated Daly, this is not surprising.

Anaconda, 1887. *BSB.*

ground in 1883 on a copper smelter and built the town of Anaconda. His mining empire ultimately broke the stranglehold of Michigan and Swansea on the nineteenth-century copper industry.

In 1899, Haggin retired, and Daly became president of the renamed Amalgamated Copper Mining Company. His new fellow directors, Henry H. Rogers and William A. Rockefeller, were both affiliated with the Standard Oil Trust (Standard Oil had no direct ownership interest). "The Company" ultimately absorbed all the mines of Butte, conquered the world of copper, and dominated the economy and politics of Montana for decades. In 1955, the Company moved from underground to open pit mining. Atlantic Richfield Company (ARCO) purchased the Company in 1977 and then closed the Anaconda smelter in 1980 and the Berkely Pit in 1982, leaving behind a Superfund site requiring remediation in perpetuity.[373]

Ultimately, enough copper emerged from the Richest Hill on Earth that, had it all been poured into one strip, it could cover Interstate 15—which closely follows the old Montana Trail—with a four-inch-thick sheet of copper extending 450 miles from Butte to south of Salt Lake City.[374]

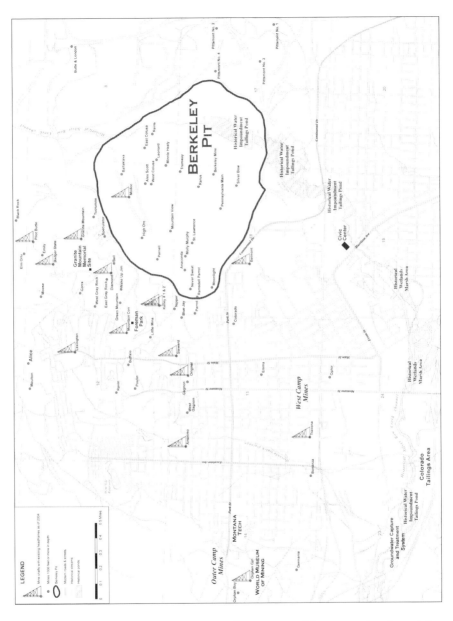

Historic location of Butte's mines superimposed over a map of the present-day city and the Berkeley Pit. Walkerville is north of the Lexington mine. *Montana Bureau of Mines and Geology.*

Daly's racehorse Montana with jockey Edward "Snapper" Garrison. *Image:* A Bay Racehorse with Jockey Up, *Henry Cross, 1892; courtesy of Hirschl and Adler Galleries, New York; photographed by Eric Baumgartner.*

Daly's fortune provided him the means to build a second empire—on the turf. In 1886, he started with an eighteen-stall barn near Anaconda, housing "two [box] carloads of blooded stock" mostly purchased from Haggin. The same year, he bought a homestead in Western Montana, south of Missoula. On lush green land, as close to Ireland as can be found in Montana, Daly platted the town of Hamilton with its lumber mill. But most of all, he fulfilled his childhood dream: his Bitter Root Stock Farm became a verdant estate with over 1,200 horses grazing the fields.

His champion racehorses soon "made a noise" as loud as any mining operation—that of roaring crowds at tracks from California to New York. His Thoroughbred manager at the Stock Farm, Sam Lucas, later declared that if Daly had not died so soon, his breeding program "would have conquered the world of turfdom."[375]

Yet the Pooka lurked. Daly lived in a time and culture in which men denied weakness. As Daly reached the peak of his power, his kidneys and heart failed, and he died on November 12, 1900. But from 1883 to 1900, the "noise" of Daly's two empires was heard throughout Montana and much of the United States as copper transformed the world.

GLOSSARY

This is a noncomprehensive list of terms that may be unfamiliar to the reader. For a comprehensive mining glossary, see *Dictionary of Mining, Mineral, and Related Terms*. U.S. Department of the Interior, 1996, republished at https://webharvest.gov/peth04/20041015011634/imcg.wr.usgs.gov/dmmrt/.

amalgamation: Use of mercury as an alloy to separate silver and gold.

arastra: A primitive mill comprising a circular, rock-lined pit in which broken ore is pulverized by heavy, flat-bottomed stones dragged by a draft animal hitched to a long horizontal pole connected to a center post.

assay: Testing an ore or mineral for composition, purity, weight, or other properties.

bullion: Metal formed into bars or ingots.

color: Gold found in streambeds.

colt: A young male horse. Inaccurately, *colt* is used interchangeably with *foal* to describe a baby horse of either sex.

concentrator: Mills and other mechanisms that mechanically separate valuable minerals from waste rock.

crosscut: A horizontal tunnel driven through a vein. *Compare* drift.

cutter: A lightweight open sleigh.

drift: A horizontal tunnel following along the length of a vein. *Compare* crosscut.

flux: Substances added during the smelting process that reduce melting temperature, separate metals from waste, and increase recovery of desired materials.

free-milling: Ore that does not require complex smelting or leaching.

gangue: Commercially worthless minerals.

grubstake: *See* stake.

headframe: The steel or timber structure at the top of a shaft that supports the cables and sheave wheels of the hoisting mechanism. Also called a gallows frame.

hoist: A mechanical device with a drum for winding rope or cable to raise and lower workers and materials in a shaft.

leaching: Using chemicals and water to dissolve out valuable minerals.

lode: A deposit of valuable minerals contained within a rock formation. *Compare* placer.

matte: Smelted product that still contains impurities.

ore: Natural rock or sediment that contains valuable minerals.

placer: A surface deposit of clay, sand, and/or gravel containing valuable minerals. Mined using water to separate minerals from waste material. *Compare* lode.

plunger: A gambler or speculator who takes bold or reckless risks.

raise: A mine opening driven upward to develop a vein or connect to an upper level for access or ventilation. (A downward inclined shaft to develop a vein below the lowest working level is a winze.)

reduction: A generic term for mechanical and chemical processes that separate metals in ore from waste materials.

refining: The final process of purifying smelted metal. Chemical and electrolytic processes used vary, depending on the materials involved.

shaft: A vertical or steeply inclined opening into a mine (horizontal openings are adits).

smelting: Applying heat and flux to ore in order to separate metal from waste.

square-set timbering: A system supporting weak rock using large timbers assembled in interconnected boxes.

stake: (1) Legally locating a mining claim, literally placing stakes into the ground to indicate boundaries. (2) Supplies or funds of a mining prospector (var. *grubstake*).

stamp mill: A machine with heavy metal "shoes" or "stamps" attached to rods, with a camshaft that lifts and drops to crush ore by pounding, preparing it for further processing.

stope: Working areas of a mine where ore is or has been extracted.

sump: The lowest point in mines, where water accumulates to be pumped out.

tailings: Sandy or powdery waste rock deposits produced by ore processing.

Thoroughbred: A horse breed developed in the British Isles, used for racing. Commonly but incorrectly used as a synonym for purebred animals of any breed.

timber (mining): (1) Using wood for supports in a mine. (2) The completed supports in place.

trotter: (1) A harness horse that races at a trot, an intermediate speed two-beat horse gait. (2) A generic term for harness racing horses.

tunnel: (1) A horizontal bore through rock that goes completely through the formation, such as a railroad tunnel. (2) A generic term for horizontal passages in a mine.

whim: A capstan or similar winding device used to hoist ore and other materials from mines. Powered by equines or oxen hitched to radiating beams.

windlass: A cylinder around which rope or cable is wound, turned by a hand crank. Used to raise and lower heavy objects.

NOTES

Preface

1. Toole, "Marcus Daly," i–v, 202.
2. Historical Company, *American Turf*, 178–209; Toole, "History of the Anaconda," 65.

Introduction

3. O'Farrell, *Butte*, 9.
4. Emmons, *American Pale*, 278
5. P.A. O'Farrell, "Notes from America," *Freeman's Gazette*, December 27, 1894.
6. *Butte Miner*, October 21, 1882, quoting *Salt Lake Tribune*, September 17, 1882.
7. *Anaconda Standard*, September 3, 1907; *Western News*, September 4, 1907. First known public reference to Butte as "The Richest Hill on Earth" *Butte Miner*, October 10, 1906; Workers, *Copper Camp*, 130, 214.
8. *New York Times*, April 26, 1903; Daly Probate, 1901; Toole, "History of the Anaconda," 65; Emmons, *Butte Irish*, 52–53; Emmons, *American Pale*, 270–71, 277–78.
9. *Anaconda Standard*, November 1, 1895.
10. *Great Falls Tribune*, November 13, 1900; *Anaconda Standard*, November 13, 1900; J.S. Cameron, "Bright's Disease Today: The Pathogenesis and Treatment of Glomerulonephritis," *British Medical Journal* 4, no. 5832 (1972): 87–90.
11. *Anaconda Standard*, November 16, 1900.
12. *Ravalli Republican*, November 16, 1900, January 2, 1901; *Anaconda Standard*, November 13, 1900; Malone, *Battle for Butte*, 18; Toole, "Marcus Daly," iv, 3, 21.
13. *Los Angeles Times*, February 28, 1897; *Anaconda Standard*, November 16, 1900.

14. Toole, "History of the Anaconda," 125–26.

15. Emmons, *Butte Irish*, 24–25, 147; Emmons, *American Pale*, 270–72; George Everett, "From the Emerald Isle to the Copper Mines," *Irish America Magazine*, August–September 2000, 84–87; Reilly video, 15:26.

16. *Butte Miner*, September 20, 1885; *Anaconda Standard*, November 14, 1900, November 22, 1900.

17. *Butte Miner*, March 17, 1898.

18. *Anaconda Standard*, September 4, 1889; Malone, *Battle for Butte*, 58, 62–63; MacMillan, *Smoke Wars*, 6, 24-32, 85, 262 note 31; Quivic, "Smoke and Tailings," 206–15; Montana Constitutional Convention, *Proceedings and Debates of the Constitutional Convention: Held in the City of Helena, Montana, July 4ᵗʰ, 1889, August 17ᵗʰ, 1889* (Helena, MT: State Publishing Company, 1921), 754.

19. U.S. federal census, 1900; Senate testimony 1900, 2204, 2212; *In re Daly's Estate* 178 misc. 943, 36 N.Y.S.2d 954 (1942); Lindsay, *Amazing Experiences*, 80.

20. Luke 12:34*;* Toole, "History of the Anaconda," 65.

21. *Montana Standard*, May 25, 1941; Gibson, "Episode 269: Marcus Daly Statue," *Verdigris.*

22. *Montana Standard*, July 15, 1941.

23. Jeffrey O'Gara, "Anaconda: The Smelter Shuts Down and So Does the Town," *High Country News*, November 14, 1980; Rich Ecke, "The Day the Anaconda Co. Stack Fell 34 Years Ago," *Great Falls Tribune*, September 11, 2016; Our Lady of the Rockies, "The Story of Our Lady," https://www.ourladyoftherockies.com/about.html.

Chapter 1

24. Daly, *Biography*, 2; Lewis, "Cavan (County of)," in *Topographical Dictionary*, 314–18.

25. *Anaconda Standard*, July 31, 1897; *Butte Inter Mountain*, March 8, 1909; *Butte Miner*, March 9, 1909; *Butte Miner*, September 28, 1919; "Marcus Daly, 60, Investment Aide," *New York Times*, July 26, 1969; "Monmouth Park Freeholder Daly Dies," *Asbury Park Press*, July 25, 1969; *In the Matter of the Estate of Kate Rudden, deceased,* no. 837, Montana Third Judicial District Court, Deer Lodge County (1913); Daly Probate, 1901; U.S. federal census, 1850, 1860, 1870, 1880 and 1900; Crosserlough parish records 1843–76; Ireland, Catholic Parish Registers, 1655–1918, via Ancestry.com; Crosserlough Parish, Ireland, cemetery records; Headstone photographs via findagrave.com; Ireland 1901 and 1911 census for Derrylea, http://www.census.nationalarchives.ie; Daly, *Biography*, 2; Malone, *Battle for Butte*, 18; Marcosson, *Anaconda*, 41–42; Sanders, *History of Montana*, 477–78; Owen Daly family history, Kevin Daly and Rosemary Daly Marcuss email correspondence, April 2021.

26. *Anaconda Standard*, November 13, 1900; Griffith's valuation; Lewis, "Cavan (County of)," in *Topographical Dictionary*, 314–18; Northern Mine Research Society, "Connaught Coalfield," https://www.nmrs.org.uk/mines-map/coal-mining-in-the-british-isles/ireland/connaught/; Concepta McGovern email, April 7, 2022.

27. Cemetery records, Crosserlough Parish.

28. Marcosson, *Anaconda*, 41.

29. Cavan County Museum, "Boat Room," http://www.cavanmuseum.ie/Default.aspx?StructureID_str=17; Our Irish Heritage, "La Téne Stones," https://www.ouririshheritage.org/content/archive/place/miscellaneous-place/la-tene-stones.

30. Gregory Wright, "Lugh," *Mythopedia*; Oxford University Press, "Enbarr: Oxford Reference"; Mac Cana, "Celtic Religion," 1,487, 1,491; MacLeod, *Celtic Myth*, 63; Feehan, *Farming in Ireland*, 189.

31. *Butte Miner*, September 3, 1907; *Anaconda Standard*, October 17, 1927; Feehan, *Farming in Ireland*, 189; Oxford University Press, "Liath Macha: Oxford Reference"; Mac Cana, "Celtic Religion," 1,491; Mac Cana, "Goddesses," 85–94; MacLeod, *Celtic Myth*, 10, 47, 50, 63; Moody, *Irish History*, 38–40; Anne Williams, "Cú Chuliann," *Mythopedia*.

32. T.W. Rolleston, et al., *The High Deeds of Finn and other Bardic Romances of Ancient Ireland* (New York: Thomas Y. Crowell & Company, Gutenberg eBook, 2005), unpaginated.

33. Bob Curran, "The Pooka," in *A Field Guide to Irish Fairies* (San Francisco, CA: Chronicle Books, 1998), 37–41; Oxford University Press, "Pooka: Oxford Reference."

34. Sir William Temple, "An Essay Upon the Advancement of Trade in Ireland," in *The Works of Sir William Temple*, vol. 3 (London: S. Hamilton, Weybridge, 1814), 20.

35. Daly, *Biography*, 2.

36. *Sheffield and Rotherham Independent*, December 23, 1892; B.K. Monroe, "1941-era Bitter Rooters Didn't Have to Worry About the Fate of the Stock Farm," *Ravalli Republic*, March 31, 1978.

37. Shoebotham, *Anaconda*, 153.

38. Robertson, *History of Thoroughbred Racing*, 146; Historical Company, *American Turf*, 179; Powell, *Dalys*, 102, 107; Powell, *Copper*, 2–4.

39. Kohrs, *Autobiography*, 96.

40. Moody, *Irish History*, 230; Loughanleagh & Muff Heritage Trust, "Fair of Muff," http://www.loughanleagh.com/fair-of-muff/; Marese McDonagh, "Fairgoers in a Huff at Muff as Rain Dampens Spirits," *Independent.ie*, August 12, 2011; Daniel Melia, interview, February 5, 2022.

41. *Anglo Celt*, April 24, 1886; Griffin, "More Sport the Merrier," 93–94; Rouse, *Sport and Ireland*, 103–4.

42. Emmons, *American Pale*, 270–72.

43. Donald M. MacRaild and Malcolm Smith, "Migration and Emigration 1600–1945," in *Ulster Since 1600: Politics, Economy, and Society* (Oxford, UK: Oxford University Press, 2013), 140–43; Moody, *Irish History*, 163–66, 188–89.

44. Daly, *Biography*, 2; Moody, *Irish History*, 173–74; Woulfe, "*Irish Names*."

45. Cusack, *Illustrated History*, 576–77; Moody, *Irish History*, 187–91, 217; *John J. Burns Library Blog*, "The Penal Laws in Ireland," October 22, 2018, https://johnjburnslibrary.wordpress.com/2018/10/22/the-penal-laws-in-ireland/.

46. Patrick Weston Joyce, "Catholic Emancipation," in *A Concise History of Ireland* (Dublin, IE: M.H. Gill and Son, 1912), 292–95; Malone, *Battle for Butte*, 18; Nathaniel Vincent Mohatt, et al. "Historical Trauma as Public Narrative," *Social Science & Medicine* 106 (2014): 128–136; Moody, *Irish History*, 241; Woodham-Smith, *Great Hunger*, 27–28.

47. John Conlan, "Robert Emmet Literary Association, Part 3," *Harp Without the Crown*, KMBF, http://www.butteamericaradio.org/news/2021/6/21/the-harp-without-the-crown-robert-emmet-literary-association-part-3; Daly, *Biography*, 2; Emmons, *Butte Irish*, 21; Reilly video, 0:19:16–0:21:50; Woulfe, "*Irish Names*."

48. Marcosson, *Anaconda*, 37; Malone, *Battle for Butte*, 18; Toole, "Marcus Daly," 2–3.

49. Reilly video; 0:19:16–0:21:50

50. *Anaconda Standard*, July 31, 1897; Phelim P. Boyle and Cormac Ó Gráda, "Fertility Trends, Excess Mortality, and the Great Irish Famine," *Demography* 23, no. 4 (November 1986): 543–62, 555, https://researchrepository.ucd.ie/bitstream/10197/401/3/ogradac_article_pub_096.pdf; Ó Murchadha, *Great Famine*, 135; Ross, *History of a Nation*, 226.

51. Foster, *Modern Ireland*, 379–83; Mitchel, *History of Ireland*, 546.

52. Griffin, "More Sport the Merrier," 91–92; Mitchel, *History of Ireland*, 543–59; Cavan County Museum, "The Great Famine," https://web.archive.org/web/20210614015208/http://www.cavanmuseum.ie/the-great-famine.htm; Woodham-Smith, *Great Hunger*, 75.

53. Montana Newspaper Association inserts, *Augusta News*, August 1, 1922; Shoebotham, *Anaconda*, 177.

54. Griffith's valuation; Reilly video, 0:19:16–0:21:50.

55. Ó Murchadha, *Great Famine*, 83; Aengus O. Snodaigh, "Remembering the Past: An Droch Shaol, the Irish Holocaust," *An Phoblacht*, August 28, 1997; Woodham-Smith, *Great Hunger*, 28; Emmons, correspondence, April 17, 2020.

56. Beretta correspondence, December 14, 2021; Dunne correspondence January 26, 2022; Emmons correspondence, April 17, 2020; Culture Northern Ireland, "Ceili Houses," https://www.culturenorthernireland.org/article/1272/ceili-houses; Griffith's valuation; Lexico, "'Strong Farmer' definition," https://www.lexico.com/en/definition/strong_farmer; Michael Quigley, "Farmers, Merchants and Priests: The Rise of the Agrarian Petty-Bourgeoisie in Ireland,

1850–85," PhD diss., McMaster University, 1980, iii, 14, 28, 47, 240; Reilly correspondence, December 12, 2021.

57. Emmons, *Butte Irish*, 21; B.E. Stack, letter, 1933, "Marcus Daly," vertical file, MHS; Senate testimony 1900, 2212.

58. Donald H. Akenson, *The Irish Education Experiment: The National System of Education in the Nineteenth Century* (New York: Routledge, 1970, reprint, 2012), 276; Concepta McGovern, email, April 7, 2022; Cormac O'Grada, "The Population of Ireland 1700–1900: A Survey," in *Annales de Démographie Historique* (1979): 283; Toole, "Marcus Daly," iv, 3; Tom Walsh, "The National System of Education, 1831–2000" in *Essays in the History of Irish Education* (London: Palgrave Macmillan Limited, 2016), 8–9, 14, 16; Encyclopedia.com, "Primary Public Education—National Schools from 1831," https://www.encyclopedia.com/ international/encyclopedias-almanacs-transcripts-and-maps/education-primary-public-education-national-schools-1831; Central Statistics Office, "Census of Population 2016 - Profile 3, An Age Profile of Ireland," https://www.cso.ie/en/ releasesandpublications/ep/p-cp3oy/cp3/agr/; Oireachtas Library and Research Service, "Education in Ireland," *Houses of the Oireachtas*, 2020, https://data. oireachtas.ie/ie/oireachtas/libraryResearch/2020/2020-04-03_l-rs-infographic-education-in-ireland-a-statistical-snapshot_en.pdf. Ireland's population in 1851 was 6.5 million, with a school enrollment of 520,401. The Republic of Ireland's 2016 population was 6.6 million, and its 2016–17 enrollment was listed with 558,314 children in primary school and 357,408 in secondary school.

59. Daly, *Biography*, 3.

60. *Gold Hill Daily News*, November 2, 1865; *Mercantile Guide and Directory for Virginia City, Gold Hill, Silver City and American City, 1864–65* (San Francisco: Agnew and Deffebach 1864), 31–32; Villanova University, "Fenian Brotherhood."

61. *Butte Miner*, June 23, 1883, October 17, 1886, October 20, 1886; *Freeman's Journal*, September 29, 1886; *Livingston Enterprise*, October 2, 1886; Egan, *Immortal Irishman*, 309–10; Emmons, *Butte Irish*, 21; Malone, *Battle for Butte*, 80–81.

62. Emmons, *Butte Irish*, 21, 51–54, 108.

63. Daly, *Biography*, 3.

64. Cusack, *Illustrated History*, 161; Mitchel, *History of Ireland*, 615–17.

65. Emmons, *Butte Irish*, 1; Miller, *Emigrants and Exiles*, 570.

Chapter 2

66. *Dictionary of American Biography*, "Marcus Daly"; Toole, "Marcus Daly," 4.

67. Egan, *Immortal Irishman*, 163; Emmons, *Butte Irish*, 1.

68. Lorraine Boissoneault, "How the 19th-Century Know-Nothing Party Reshaped American Politics," *Smithsonian Magazine*, January 26, 2017; Mark Bulik, "1854:

No Irish Need Apply," *New York Times*, September 8, 2015; Sheila Langan, "'No Irish Need Apply' Signs Existed Despite Denials, High Schooler Proved," *Irish Central*, April 8, 2021.

69. *Anaconda Standard*, July 2, 1922; Montana Newspaper Association Inserts, May 15, 1941, "Marcus Daly" Vertical File, MHS.

70. "Our Japanese Village," *Puck* 18, no. 462 (January 13, 1886), centerfold image, "Cartoons and Comments," 306. The cartoon that depicted Daly caricatured various public figures using imagery from the Gilbert and Sullivan play *The Mikado*, popular at the time.

71. "Daly Estate Horse Sale," *New York Times*, December 25, 1900.

72. Emmons, *Butte Irish*, 19; John Killick, "Transatlantic Steerage Fares, British and Irish Migration, and Return Migration, 1815–60," *Economic History Review* 67, no. 1 (February 2014): 175, 178, 182; Marcosson, *Anaconda*, 42.

73. O'Hanlon, *Emigrants Guide*, 26, 33–36.

74. Ibid., 19–21, 25–29, 40.

75. Ibid., 26, 33–36.

76. Ibid., 19–21; Brian Murphy, *Adrift* (New York: Da Capo Press, 2018), ii, 16, 26; Svejda, "Castle Garden," 14–17.

77. O'Hanlon, *Emigrants Guide*, 19–29.

78. National Park Service, "History and Culture," Castle Clinton National Monument, https://www.nps.gov/cacl/learn/historyculture/index.htm; O'Hanlon, *Emigrants Guide*, 19–29, 40–45; Kathryn Stephenson, "The Quarantine War: The Burning of the New York Marine Hospital in 1858," *Public Health Reports* 119, no. 1 (January–February 2004): 79–92; Svejda, "Castle Garden," 32–35; Woodham-Smith, *Great Hunger*, 254.

79. U.S. federal census, 1850, New Haven, CT; *Anaconda Standard*, July 31, 1897; Daly, *Biography*, 3; John Grenham, "Irish Roots: Chain Migration—'Nobody Ever Left Ireland to Go to America,'" *Irish Times*, September 2, 2014.

80. U.S. federal census, 1860, township 3, Placer County, CA; *Ravalli Republican*, January 2, 1901; Powell, *Dalys*, 5.

81. *New York Times*, November 13, 1900; *Ravalli Republican*, January 2, 1901; *Montana Standard*, May 23, 1937; *Montana Standard*, July 21, 1950; Daly, *Biography*, 3; *Progressive Men*, 16; Malone, *Battle for Butte*, 18–19; Marcosson, *Anaconda*, 42; Powell, *Dalys*, 5–6; Sanders, *History of Montana*, 477; Shoebotham, *Anaconda*, 177–78; Toole, "Marcus Daly," 3.

82. *New York Times*, November 13, 1900; Cummings, *American and His Food*, 242–46; Egan, *Immortal Irishman*, 132; D.A. Levy, ed., "Cost of Passage," Maritime Heritage Project, https://www.maritimeheritage.org/news/costOfPassage.html; Joseph D. Weeks, "Report on the Statistics of Wages in Manufacturing Industries," Washington, D.C.: Government Printing Office, 1886; Western Economic Society, "Unskilled Labor in the United States," *Journal of Political Economy* 13 (1905): 356.

83. McShane and Tarr, *Horse in the City*, 97–100.

84. Malone, *Battle for Butte*, 19; O'Hanlon, *Emigrants Guide*, 47.

85. O'Hanlon, *Emigrants Guide*, 45–46.

86. Golway, *Machine Made*, xviii, xix, 2, 43, 45–46, 201.

87. Tyler Anbinder, *Five Points: The 19th Century New York City Neighborhood that Invented Tap Dance, Stole Elections, and Became the World's Most Notorious Slum* (New York: Simon and Schuster, 2001), 289; Golway, *Machine Made*, 53–56; J.T. Headley, *Pen and Pencil Sketches of the Great Riots* (New York: E.B. Treat, 1877), 129–35.

88. Golway, *Machine Made*, 55–59; Riordon, *Plunkitt*, 3, 10, 170–73.

89. Riordon, *Plunkitt*, 170–73.

90. Toole, "History of the Anaconda," 56–65.

91. Department of the Taoiseach. "The National Flag," November 1, 2018, https://www.gov.ie/en/publication/adc448-the-national-flag/; Egan, *Immortal Irishman*, 143.

92. Egan, *Immortal Irishman*, 159, 163; Emmons, *Butte Irish*, 51–54; Library of Congress, "The Irish News," https://www.loc.gov/item/sn83030202/; Library of Congress, "The Irish World and American Industrial Liberator," https://www.loc.gov/item/sn83030537/.

93. *Anaconda Standard*, March 17, 1898; Egan, *Immortal Irishman*, 309–10; Emmons, *Butte Irish*, 21, 118–19.

94. Greene, *Horses at Work*, 43–45, 174–76; McShane and Tarr, *Horse in the City*, 52, 85; Morris, "Horse Power," 43.

95. Greene, *Horses at Work*, 174–76, 241; Morris, "Horse Power," 43.

96. Adelman, "First Modern Sport," 8, 11; International Museum of the Horse, "Golden Age of the Trotting Horse," http://imh.org/exhibits/online/legacy-of-the-horse/golden-age-trotting-horse/.

97. Adelman, "First Modern Sport," 15–16; McShane and Tarr, *Horse in the City*, 93; Powell, *Copper*, 95.

98. Adelman, "First Modern Sport," 18–21.

99. McShane and Tarr, *Horse in the City*, 90–92, 114.

100. Egan, *Immortal Irishman*, 172–77, 190–91; Mitchel, *History of Ireland*, 621; New York Historical Society, "King Cotton," New York Divided, https://web.archive.org/web/20130330070752/http://nydivided.org/VirtualExhibit/T1/G1/G1ReadMore.php.

Chapter 3

101. *Anaconda Standard*, July 31, 1897; Daly, *Biography*, 4; Malone, *Battle for Butte*, 18; Marcosson, *Anaconda*, 42, Toole, "Marcus Daly," 4; U.S. federal census, 1860, Placer County, CA.

102. *Gold Hill Daily News*, November 2, 1865; *Montana Standard*, July 21, 1950.

103. Bethel, "Golden Skein," 250–56; Crouch, *Bonanza King*, 133; Daly, *Biography*, 4; Everhart, *Mining Frontier*, 7, 9; Lindsay, *Amazing Experiences*, 99; Marcosson, *Anaconda*, 42; Nickliss, *Phoebe Apperson Hearst*, 34; Powell, *Dalys*, 5; LOC, "The Forty-Niners" in *California as I Saw It*; Smithsonian Institution, "To California by Sea," https://americanhistory.si.edu/onthewater/exhibition/2_4.html; U.S. Department of the Interior, National Park Service, "California's Role in the Civil War," Golden Gate National Recreation Area, https://www.nps.gov/goga/learn/historyculture/california-in-civil-war.htm.

104. Brewer and Farquhar, *Up and Down California*, 3–9; Fessenden N. Otis, *Illustrated History of the Panama Railroad* (New York, Harper and Brothers, 1862), 147–48; Lynda M. Reid, "A Brief But Curious History of Horse Racing in Panama—Part I," *Silver People Heritage Foundation*, September 28, 2009, https://thesilverpeopleheritage.wordpress.com/2009/09/28/a-brief-but-curious-history-of-horse-racing-in-panama---part-i/.

105. Brewer and Farquhar, *Up and Down California*, 6–9; Biggest U.S. Cities, "Top 100 Biggest US Cities in The Year 1860," https://www.biggestuscities.com/1860; LOC, "Government and Law" in *California as I Saw It*.

106. Daly, *Biography*, 4; Loomis, *Wells Fargo*, 58; Emmons, *American Pale*, 213, 320; Nickliss, *Phoebe Apperson Hearst*, 35–37; Rudolph F. Lapp, "Negro Rights Activities in Gold Rush California," *California Historical Society Quarterly*, March 1966; Calisphere, "Gold Rush Era to 1900," https://calisphere.org/exhibitions/47/african-americans-gold-rush/; Leslie M. Harris, "African-Americans in New York City, 1626–1863," *Emory University Department of History Newsletter*, no. 26 (August 2001); *Historical Statistics of the United States, Colonial Times to 1870* (Washington, D.C.: Bureau of the Census, 1975), 25.

107. Clayton, Hoy, and Underwood, *Vaqueros, Cowboys, and Buckaroos*, xv–xvii, 2–10, 209; Cowdrey, Martin and Martin, *Horses & Bridles*, 8–10; NARA, "Land Grands and Claims"; LOC, "Mexican California" in *California as I Saw It*.

108. Julian Brave NoiseCat, "We are Still Here," *Nation*, January 24, 2022; Edward D. Castillo, "Short Overview of California Indian History," California Native American Heritage Commission, 2002, https://nahc.ca.gov/resources/california-indian-history/; LOC, "First Peoples of California," "Spanish California," "The Missions," "From Gold Rush to Golden State," and "Government and Law " in *California as I Saw It*; Joshua Paddison, "Before 1768: Pre-Columbian California," Calisphere, https://calisphere.org/exhibitions/essay/1/pre-columbian/; William Preston, "Serpent in Eden: Dispersal of Foreign Diseases into Pre-Mission California," *Journal of California and Great Basin Anthropology* 18, no. 1 (1996): 2–37; Tarin Luna, "Newsom Apologizes for California's History of Violence Against Native Americans," *Los Angeles Times*, June 18, 2019.

109. Colton, *Three Years*, 37–38; Brian McGinty, "Colton Hall, Constitutional Cradle," *American Bar Association Journal* (June 1973): 641–43.

110. Colton, *Three Years*, 20; Malone, *Battle for Butte*, 19; Kristin Mann, "The Musical Tradition in Latin America," *Oxford Bibliographies*, August 13, 2015; Powell, *Dalys*, 30; Robertson, *History of Thoroughbred Racing*, 81–82.

111. NARA, "Land Grands and Claims"; *More v. Steinbach*, 127 U.S. 70 (1888) illustrates the complex land claim adjudication process.

112. Carlisle, "Hearst"; Swanberg, *Citizen Hearst*, 5, 9, 13; Nasaw, *Chief*, 7; Nickliss, *Phoebe Apperson Hearst*, 27, 30–31.

113. Crouch, *Bonanza King*, 60–63, 67–69, 433; Jung, "Capitalism Comes," 69; Marcosson, *Anaconda*, 37; Morris, *Lighting Out*, 103; William Wright (Dan De Quille), *History of the Big Bonanza* (Hartford, CT: American Publishing Company, 1877), 54.

114. Nasaw, *Chief*, 4–8; Marcosson, *Anaconda*, 37; Nickliss, *Phoebe Apperson Hearst*, 16–18, 23–27, 32–38; Carlisle, "Hearst."

115. Nickliss, *Phoebe Apperson Hearst*, 38–43; Nasaw, *Chief*, 4–8.

116. *San Francisco Call*, July 25, 1899; Sergent, "Pastime of Millions," 48–55; Phelps, *California's Representative Men*, 27–31, 328; Lawrence James Jelinek, "Property of Every Kind: Ranching and Framing During the Gold Rush Era," in *A Golden State*, 237.

117. *Mississippi Free Trader*, July 3, 1850; Harrison, *Progressive Americans*, 145–49; Marcosson, *Anaconda*, 34; Phelps, *California's Representative Men*, 325; Sergent, "Pastime of Millions," 37–44, 48–51.

118. *Mississippi Free Trader*, January 18, 1851; Bethel, "Golden Skein," 251–54; Sergent, "Pastime of Millions," 64.

119. *Mississippi Free Trader*, July 3, 1850; *San Francisco Examiner*, July 25, 1899; Patrick J. Furlong, "Haggin, James Ben Ali," *American National Biography*; Lexington History Museum, "James Ben Ali Haggin," http://lexhistory.org/wikilex/james-ben-ali-haggin; Marcosson, *Anaconda*, 33; Phelps, *California's Representative Men*, 28–30; Sergent, "Pastime of Millions," 48–55.

120. Loomis, *Wells Fargo*, 204; Phelps, *California's Representative Men*, 28; Sergent, "Pastime of Millions," 38, 55, 119; Oscar Tully Shuck, *Bench and Bar in California: History, Anecdotes, Reminiscences* (San Francisco, CA: Occident Printing House, 1889), 247–48; Toole, "Marcus Daly," 78–82.

121. Toole, "Marcus Daly," 80–81.

122. Marcosson, *Anaconda*, 33–34; Sergent, "Pastime of Millions," 57; Smith, *History of the Comstock*, 84.

123. Carlisle, "Hearst"; Loomis, *Wells Fargo*, 204; Montgomery, *Thoroughbred*, 162; Phelps, *California's Representative Men*, 28; Robertson, *History of Thoroughbred Racing*, 112; California State Parks, "Hearst San Simeon State Park and Historical Monument," https://www.parks.ca.gov/pages/590/files/HearstSanSimeonFinalWeb2015.pdf.

124. "The Passing of Rancho Del Paso," *New York Times*, October 8, 1905; Sergent, "Pastime of Millions," 19, 26, 96, 99–100, 116; Toole, "Marcus Daly," 33; Toole, "History of the Anaconda," 17.

125. "Irrigation and Enterprise," *Breeder and Sportsman*, September 9, 1899, 168–69; "Cholly Francisco Observes," *San Francisco Examiner*, March 19, 1946; Verne R. Albright, *The Tevis Cup* (Los Gatos, CA: Forge Valley Books, 1969), 3, 7–8; Christopher Corbett, *Orphans Preferred* (New York: Broadway Books, 2003), 187–90, 195; Igler, *Industrial Cowboys*, 101–3; Loomis, *Wells Fargo*, 204; Phelps, *California's Representative Men*, 28; Raymond W. Settle, *Saddles and Spurs: The Pony Express Saga* (Harrisburg, PA: Stackpole Co., 1955), 185–86; Sergent, "Pastime of Millions," 74, 117; *Lux v. Haggin*, 69 Cal. 255 (Cal. 1886).

126. *Sacramento Bee*, March 16, 1866; U.S. federal census, 1860, township 3, Placer County, CA; U.S. federal census, 1870, Storey County, Virginia City, NV; Historic Hwy 49, "Auburn History," http://www.historichwy49.com/aubhist.html; Loomis, *Wells Fargo*, 67; Tracy Thornton, "St. Patrick's Cemetery Angel a Symbol of Resilience," *Montana Standard*, September 13, 2020; Montana, U.S., county marriages, 1865–1987, Marcus O'Farrell, Lewis and Clark County marriage records, vol. 1–2, C-D 1887–94, no. 794, October 9, 1890.

127. "Death of a California Pioneer," *Placer Herald*, July 7, 1866; Michael Ritter, *Jean Baptiste Charbonneau, Man of Two Worlds* (Charleston, SC: Booksurge, 2005), 136, 176.

128. Crouch, *Bonanza King*, 34; Jung, "Capitalism Comes," 52–77; Elijah Robinson Kennedy, *The Contest for California in 1861: How Colonel E.D. Baker Saved the Pacific States to the Union* (Boston: Houghton Mifflin Company, 1912), 1–3.

129. *San Francisco Call*, May 7, 1893; *Anaconda Standard*, November 13, 1900; Daly, *Biography*, 4; Freeman, *Brief History*, 43; Marcosson, *Anaconda*, 42; Toole, "Marcus Daly," 3–4.

130. National Oceanic and Atmospheric Administration, "What Are Atmospheric Rivers?" https://www.noaa.gov/stories/what-are-atmospheric-rivers; Newbold, "Great California Flood," 1–2; Philpott, "Biblical Flood."

131. Brewer and Farquhar, *Up and Down California*, 241–44, 295; Crouch, *Bonanza King*, 133; Newbold, "Great California Flood," 3–6; Philpott, "Biblical Flood."

132. Brewer and Farquhar, *Up and Down California*, 241–44, 295; Newbold, "Great California Flood," 3–5; Philpott, "Biblical Flood."

133. *Adams v. Norris*, 64 U.S. 353 (1859); *Norris v. Haggin*, 136 U.S. 386 (1890); Allen L. Chickering, "Samuel Norris: Litigious Pioneer," *California Historical Society Quarterly* 25, no. 3 (1946): 219–28; Malone, *Battle for Butte*, 19; Newbold, "Great California Flood," 6–7; Sergent, "Pastime of Millions," 93–97.

134. Hittell, *Gold Mines and Mining*, 11–12, 19–20, 24; Jung, "Capitalism Comes," 59–63; Newbold, "Great California Flood," 1.

135. Crouch, *Bonanza King*, 40; Everhart, *Mining Frontier*, 10; Hittell, *Gold Mines and Mining*, 44–45.

136. *Butte Miner*, May 20, 1903; *Anaconda Standard*, May 20, 1903; Malone, *Battle for Butte*, 18–19; Powell, *Dalys*, 6; Toole, "Marcus Daly," 4.

137. *Nebraska State Journal*, November 19, 1900 (reprint from unknown New York newspaper); Daly, *Biography*, 4; Malone, *Battle for Butte*, 18–19; Marcosson, *Anaconda*, 36, 42; Shoebotham, *Anaconda*, 15; Historic Hwy 49, "Angel's Camp," http://www.historichwy49.com/angel/angel.html.

138. *Sacramento Bee*, January 23, 1866; Crouch, *Bonanza King*, 40, 137, 211; Daly, *Biography*, 19; Malone, *Battle for Butte*, 18–19; Marcosson, *Anaconda*, 36, 42; Shoebotham, *Anaconda*, 15.

139. *Louisville Courier-Journal*, July 10, 1899 (reprint from the *San Francisco Bulletin*); Daly, *Biography*, 19.

140. Go Calaveras, "Calaveras County History," https://www.gocalaveras.com/history/; Rebecca Robbins Raines, *Getting the Message Through: A Branch History of the U.S. Army Signal Corps*, Army Historical Series (Washington, D.C.: United States Army Center of Military History, 1996), 13–14, 17.

141. *Contra Costa Gazette*, January 28, 1865, April 1, 1865; *Anaconda Standard*, November 1, 1895; Freeman, *Brief History*, 17; Gibson, "Episode 191: Montana Copper Company," *Verdigris*; Malone, *Battle for Butte*, 61.

142. *Louisville Courier-Journal*, July 10, 1899 (reprint from the *San Francisco Bulletin*); *Salt Lake Herald Republican*, November 14, 1900; Hittell, *Gold Mines and Mining*, 42–54; Lindsay, *Amazing Experiences*, 99; Malone, *Battle for Butte*, 18–19; Shoebotham, *Anaconda*, 15.

143. *Ravalli Republican*, November 16, 1900; Lindsay, *Amazing Experiences*, 67, 74.

144. Crouch, *Bonanza King*, 33; Lucile Eaves, *A History of California Labor Legislation* (Berkeley: University of California Press, 1910), 324–25; Lunsford, "Take a Chance"; Hamilton Wright, "The Sport of Roping Grizzlies in California's Early Days," *San Francisco Call*, January 15, 1911.

145. Mary Fleming, *A History of the Thoroughbred in California* (Los Angeles: Sinclair Printing and the California Thoroughbred Breeders Association, 1983), 1–2; Lunsford, "Take a Chance."

146. Crouch, *Bonanza King*, 34, 197; Emmons, *American Pale*, 31–35; Greene, *Horses at Work*, 214; Hittell, *Gold Mines and Mining*, 47; McShane and Tarr, *Horse in the City*, 18, 20; *Transactions of the Federated Institution of Mining Engineers*, vol. 15 (Newcastle-Upon-Tyne, UK: Federated Institution of Mining Engineers, Great Britain, January 1898), 558–60.

147. Shoebotham, *Anaconda*, 175–76.

Chapter 4

148. Crouch, *Bonanza King*, 332, 364, 380, 433; United States Mint, "Timeline of the United States Mint: 1800s," https://www.usmint.gov/learn/history/timeline-of-the-united-states-mint-1800s.

149. Crouch, *Bonanza King*, 249–50; Twain, *Roughing It*, loc. 2,143. Horse prices fluctuated widely, but advertisements circa 1865 in California and Nevada suggest averages. Twain paid twenty-seven dollars for a horse.

150. Crouch, *Bonanza King*, 137, 233; Everhart, *Mining Frontier*, 30; Remi Nadeau, "Go It, Washoe!" *American Heritage* 10, no. 3 (April 1959; reprint, winter 2011); Smith, *History of the Comstock*, 17; "Lloyd Tevis," *Dictionary of American Biography*, vol. 18 (New York: Charles Scribner's Sons, 1936), 384–85.

151. Crouch, *Bonanza King*, 137, 152, 233; Daly, *Biography*, 4; Malone, *Battle for Butte*, 18–19; Marcosson, *Anaconda*, 16–17, 42; Nasaw, *Chief*, 6–7; Toole, "Marcus Daly," 4; National Park Service, "The First Ride on the Pony Express," https://www.nps.gov/articles/000/the-first-ride-on-the-pony-express.htm.

152. *Gold Hill Daily News*, November 2, 1865; Villanova University, "Fenian Brotherhood"; Connolly, "Story of Montana," 454.

153. Crouch, *Bonanza King*, 269; National Park Service, "Four Special Spikes," https://www.nps.gov/gosp/learn/historyculture/four-special-spikes.htm; V&T Railway Commission, "The Original Virginia & Truckee Railroad," https://vtrailway.com/about/history/.

154. Bernstein, *George Hearst*, 27; Crouch, *Bonanza King*, 33; Freeman, *Brief History*, 43; Glasscock, *War of the Copper Kings*, loc. 730; Lindsay, *Amazing Experiences*, 97; Malone, *Battle for Butte*, 19; Marcosson, *Anaconda*, 43; Powell, *Dalys*, 6; Toole, "Marcus Daly," 6–7.

155. *Independent Record*, May 30, 1889; Bernstein, *George Hearst*, 65; Crouch, *Bonanza King*, 237–40; Marcosson, *Anaconda*, 121; Nasaw, *Chief*, 8–9; Nickliss, *Phoebe Apperson Hearst*, 38–45, 65–67; Swanberg, *Citizen Hearst*, 7–10, 20; Turnbull, "Old Mines," 147–64; Phoebe Hearst, letter to Orrin Peck, June 24, 1896; Orrin M. Peck, correspondence and miscellany, 1860–1921, MS 1673, California Historical Society.

156. *Independent Record*, September 3, 1881, July 12, 1937; *Butte Miner*, June 13, 1883; Marcosson, *Anaconda*, 121; Powell, *Dalys*, 9; Turnbull, "Old Mines," 150, 162.

157. Historical Company, *American Turf*, 179.

158. *Ravalli Republican*, November 16, 1900; Crouch, *Bonanza King*, 127–28, 169–71; Crouch, "Mining Millionaire"; Daly, *Biography*, 4, 19; Malone, *Battle for Butte*, 18–19; Marcosson, *Anaconda*, 42; Toole, "Marcus Daly," 4–5; Toole, "History of the Anaconda," 6.

159. Crouch, *Bonanza King*, 1–7, 22–23, 170–71; 195–98.

160. Crouch, *Bonanza King*, 128, 148–49, 195–201, 255–64; Emmons, *American Pale*, 270–71; Toole, "Marcus Daly," 5.

161. *Anaconda Standard*, November 14, 1900; *Butte Inter-Mountain*, July 22, 1902; Glasscock, *War of the Copper Kings*, loc. 383–89; Marcosson, *Anaconda*, 42; Toole, "Marcus Daly," 4.

162. *Gold Hill Daily News*, December 28, 1868; *Nevada State Journal*, August 14, 1925; *Butte Miner*, August 16, 1925; Connolly, "Story of Montana," 454.

163. Crouch, *Bonanza King*, 292–93, 302–13, 327–30, 381.

164. Ibid., 127–28, 136, 151, 169–71, 175; Crouch, "Mining Millionaire"; Everhart, *Mining Frontier*, 33.

165. Crouch, *Bonanza King*, 65–66, 91, 105–9; Rickard, *History of American Mining*, 98, 101, 345.

166. Crouch, *Bonanza King*, 108–9, 114–19, 218–19, 249–50, 304, 315; M.C. Ihlsing and Eugene B. Wilson, *A Manual of Mining* (New York: John Wiley & Sons, 1911), 679–81; Douglas MacDonald, "Races, Mines and Petroglyphs," *Reno Gazette-Journal*, March 16, 1973; Marcosson, *Anaconda*, 36; Shinn, *Story of the Mine*, 227–30; Shoebotham, *Anaconda*, 17–18; Toole, "Marcus Daly," 5

167. Crouch, *Bonanza King*, 91, 109, 286; Rickard, *History of American Mining*, 98, 101, 345.

168. Crouch, *Bonanza King*, 90–102; Jerome Edwards, "Pyramid Lake War," *Online Nevada Encyclopedia*, https://www.onlinenevada.org/articles/pyramid-lake-war.

169. Crouch, *Bonanza King*, 126–27.

170. Powers, *Mark Twain*, 126; Twain, *Roughing It*, loc. 15.

171. Robert G. Cleland, "Transportation in California Before the Railroads, with Especial Reference to Los Angeles," *Annual Publication of the Historical Society of Southern California* 11, no. 1 (1918): 64–65; Mortimer M. Shelley, *Shelley's U.S. Railway, Steam Navigation and Mining Guide* (New York: Shelley's Publication House, 1865), 6–7; Twain, *Roughing It*, loc. 676–694; U.S. Postal Service, "Overland Mail to California in the 1850s," https://about.usps.com/who/profile/history/overland-mail.htm; National Postal Museum, "Overland Mail Employee's Notebook," https://postalmuseum.si.edu/collections/object-spotlight/overland-mail-employees-notebook; California State Parks, "Stagecoach History: Stage Lines to California," https://www.parks.ca.gov/?page_id=25066; History Nebraska, "Stagecoach Travel," https://history.nebraska.gov/publications/stagecoach-travel.

172. Crouch, *Bonanza King*, 154; Powers, *Mark Twain*, 126, 139–41.

173. Gillis, *Gold Rush Days*, 59; Morris, *Lighting Out*, 164–73.

174. *Gold Hill Daily News*, November 1, 1866, November 10, 1866, November 12, 1866.

175. *Gold Hill Daily News*, November 12, 1866; *Anaconda Standard*, August 4, 1895; Morris, *Lighting Out*, 222–24.

176. Malone, *Battle for Butte*, 19; Marcosson, *Anaconda*, 43; Shoebotham, *Anaconda*, 18–19. Marcosson and Shoebotham both mention the Twain holdup, but each account has errors.

177. *Great Falls Tribune*, August 3, 1895; *Chicago Tribune*, November 16, 1900; Toole, "Marcus Daly," 180; Glasscock, *War of the Copper Kings*, loc. 2453–2597; Pat Williams, "When Twain Delighted Montanans," *Missoulian*, February 23, 2010.

178. Meade, "Fall in Price," 316–39; Nolan, "Eureka Mining District," 54; Western Mining History, "Eureka, Nevada"; Western Mining History, "Pioche Nevada."

179. Nasaw, *Chief*, 23; Mark Stein, *How the States Got Their Shapes* (New York: HarperCollins, 2008), 176–177, 274.

180. Loomis, *Wells Fargo*, 199–200, 210, 215; *San Francisco Examiner*, July 25, 1899; LexHistory, "James Ben Ali Haggin," http://lexhistory.org/wikilex/james-ben-ali-haggin.

181. "White Pine and the New Route," *Daily Alta California*, January 16, 1869; Bliss, *Merchants and Miners*, 183; Malone, *Battle for Butte*, 19; Marcosson, *Anaconda*, 38–39, 43; Nasaw, *Chief*, 23; Sean Pitts, "White Pine County Experienced One of the Richest Mining Booms," *Ely Times*, February 22, 2019; Shoebotham, *Anaconda*, 21–28; Toole, "Marcus Daly," 5; Matt Weiser, "White Pine County Celebrates 150 Years," *Ely Times*, n.d., http://elynevada.net/white-pine-county-celebrates-150-years/.

182. U.S. federal census, 1870, Hamilton, White Pine, NV; Marcosson, *Anaconda*, 43; Nolan, "Eureka Mining District," 2–3; Western Mining History, "Eureka, Nevada."

183. U.S. federal census, 1870 and 1880. Marcus O'Farrell's headstone states he was born in 1871, but he appears in the 1870 census.

184. "Cornelius F. Kelley Is Dead," *New York Times*, May 13, 1957; Western Mining History, "Eureka, Nevada"; Malone, *Battle for Butte*, 19; Marcosson, *Anaconda*, vii, 27–29, 43, 68; Nolan, "Eureka Mining District," 2–3; Thomas Charles Satterthwaite, "Cornelius Francis Kelley: The Rise of an Industrial Statesman," master's thesis, Montana State University, 1971, 2–5, fn3.

185. *Salt Lake Daily Review*, October 5, 1871; James and Fell, "Alta," 277.

Chapter 5

186. *Salt Lake Herald-Republican*, June 16, 1899; Dwyer, *Story of the Cathedral*, 11.

187. *Deseret News*, March 1, 1855, February 2, 1870; *Salt Lake Tribune*, February 13, 1878.

188. Cowdrey, Martin and Martin, *Horses & Bridles*, 2, 8–10; Smithsonian Institution, "Horse Trading Among Nations" *A Song for the Horse Nation*, https://americanindian.si.edu/static/exhibitions/horsenation/trading.html; Tom Rea, "Road to Rendezvous: The Rocky Mountain Fur Trade in 1834," Wyoming State Historical Society, November 8, 2014; Samuel Western, "Trade Among Tribes: Commerce on the Plains Before Europeans Arrived," Wyoming State Historical Society, April 26, 2016.

189. Rick Graetz and Susie Graetz, "Road to Montana Teeming with Colorful History," *Independent Record*, February 7, 2006; L. Kay Edrington, "A Study of Early Utah-Montana Trade, Transportation, and Communication, 1847–1881," master's thesis, Brigham Young University, 1959, 150–51; Betty Madsen and Brigham Madsen, *North to Montana; Jehus, Bullwhackers, and Mule Skinners on the Montana Trail* (Salt Lake City: University of Utah Press, 1980), xii.

190. Bliss, *Merchants and Miners*, 32–35; Newell G. Bringhurst, "Young, Brigham," in *Utah History Encyclopedia*; Church of Jesus Christ of Latter-day Saints, "Pioneer Trek," https://newsroom.churchofjesuschrist.org/article/pioneer-trek; U.S. Census Bureau, "Historical Statistics of the United States," https://www.census.gov/history/pdf/histstats-colonial-1970.pdf.

191. Archives West, "Walker Brothers"; Bliss, *Merchants and Miners*, 13, 21–25, 28–42, 49; Markosian, Part I; Tullidge, *History of Salt Lake City*, appendix, 52–54.

192. Bliss, *Merchants and Miners*, 42–55; Tullidge, *History of Salt Lake City*, appendix, 52–53.

193. Bliss, *Merchants and Miners*, 49, 52–55, 60–66, 75–81, 102–7; Markosian, Part I; Church History Database, "Mercy Long"; Tullidge *History of Salt Lake City*, appendix, 52–54.

194. Bliss, *Merchants and Miners*, 83, 99–100, 105–7; Tullidge, *History of Salt Lake City*, appendix, 53.

195. Archives West, "Walker Brothers"; Bliss, *Merchants and Miners*, 49, 93–102, 114–21, 127–35; Markosian, Part II; Tullidge, *History of Salt Lake City*, appendix, 53–56, 246–48.

196. Bliss, *Merchants and Miners*, 138–41.

197. Ibid., 140–41, 159–60.

198. Archives West, "Walker Brothers"; Bliss, *Merchants and Miners*, 140–45; Campbell, "Saints and the Union"; Brigham D. Madsen, "Connor, Patrick Edward," in *Utah History Encyclopedia*; Nichols, "Colonel Connor"; Whitehead and Rampton, "Bingham Canyon," 220–22.

199. Daysha Eaton, "Forgotten Shoshone Massacre Story Will Soon Be Told on Grand Scale," KUER, January 31, 2019; Brigham D. Madsen, "Bear River Massacre" in *Utah History Encyclopedia*; Brigham D. Madsen, *The Shoshoni Frontier and the Bear River Massacre* (Salt Lake City: University of Utah Press, 1985), 192; Marley Madsen, "Boa Ogoi: Restoring Sacred Land 150 Years After the Bear River Massacre," *Utah State Today*, September 16, 2020, https://www.usu.edu/today/story/boa-ogoi-restoring-sacred-land-150-years-after-the-bear-river-massacre; Kristen Moulton, "Newly Uncovered Documents Claim Far Higher Number of Shoshones Killed in Bear River Massacre," *Salt Lake Tribune*, February 17, 2008.

200. Bliss, *Merchants and Miners*, 140–41; Brigham D. Madsen, "Connor, Patrick Edward," in *Utah History Encyclopedia*; Nichols, "Colonel Connor"; Philip F. Notarianni, "Forward," in *From the Ground Up*, xi; Madsen, "General Patrick

Edward Connor," 58–60; Campbell, "Saints and the Union"; Whitehead and Rampton, "Bingham Canyon," 220–22; Tullidge, *History of Salt Lake City*, 697–99; Markosian, Part II.

201. Bliss, *Merchants and Miners*, 152–55.

202. Ibid., 160–65; Martha Sontag Bradley, "Zion's Cooperative Mercantile Institution," in *Utah History Encyclopedia*; Markosian, Part II.

203. James and Fell, "Alta," 275–77; Markosian, Part II.

204. James and Fell, "Alta," 277; Markosian, Part II.

205. *Salt Lake Herald Republican*, November 14, 1900; *Butte Miner*, February 26, 1914; *Anaconda Standard*, February 26, 1914; Bliss, *Merchants and Miners*, 183; James and Fell, "Alta," 277; Toole, "Marcus Daly," 5.

206. "Daly's Mammoth Deal," *Salt Lake Herald-Republican*, June 16, 1899; Bliss, *Merchants and Miners*, 169; James and Fell, "Alta," 277–80; Marcosson, *Anaconda*, 43–44.

207. Bliss, *Merchants and Miners*, 169–75; James and Fell, "Alta," 277–82; Marcosson, *Anaconda*, 43–44.

208. Daly Probate, 1901.

209. Bliss, *Merchants and Miners*, 170–72, 176; Madsen, "General Patrick Edward Connor," 67–68; Marcosson, *Anaconda*, 44; William T. Parry, "Geology and Utah's Mineral Treasures," in *From the Ground Up*, 29–30; Rickard, *History of American Mining*, 189.

210. *Salt Lake Daily Review*, October 5, 1871; *Utah Mining Gazette*, March 14, 1874, June 6, 1874; *Salt Lake Tribune*, April 21, 1874; Bliss, *Merchants and Miners*, 176; Marcosson, *Anaconda*, 44; Sloan, *Gazetteer of Utah*, 93.

211. *Salt Lake Herald-Republican*, December 25, 1891; Bliss, *Merchants and Miners*, 177–78; Hal Compton and David Hampshire, "Park City," in *From the Ground Up*, 321–22; Marcosson, *Anaconda*, 38–39; Toole, "Marcus Daly," 6–8.

212. *Deseret News*, July 19, 1872; *Daily State Register*, August 24, 1872; *Daily Alta California*, August 27, 1872; *San Francisco Chronicle*, November 24, 1872.

213. *San Francisco Examiner*, August 26, 1872; *Chicago Inter-Ocean*, September 9, 1872; *Utah Mining Journal*, January 27, 1873; *Salt Lake Herald*, January 1, 1882; *Salt Lake Herald-Republican*, December 25, 1891; Compton and Hampshire, "Park City," 321; Malone, *Battle for Butte*, 26; Marcosson, *Anaconda*, 39; Nasaw, *Chief*, 23; Rickard, *History of American Mining*, 98, 351; Toole, "Marcus Daly," 6–7 (citing Fremont Older, *Life of George Hearst: California Pioneer* (Beverly Hills, CA: William Randolph Hearst, 1933), 127. Toole noted several inaccuracies in that work).

214. *Butte Miner*, December 13, 1881; *Independent Record*, December 22, 1882; *Helena Weekly Herald*, December 28, 1882; *Salt Lake Herald*, September 4, 1892, April 12, 1892; *Salt Lake Tribune*, April 12, 1901; Gibson, "R.C. Chambers"; Archive Record, "Jim Street Collection," BSB, https://buttearchives.pastperfectonline.com/archive/B8CEED7C-0DDB-4820-A05D-585681421270.

215. Carl J. Mayer, "The 1872 Mining Law: Historical Origins of the Discovery Rule," *University of Chicago Law Review* 53, no. 624 (1986), 624–53; Mark Squillace, "The Enduring Vitality of the General Mining Law of 1872," *Environmental Law Reporter* 18 Env. L. Rep. 10261 (1988): 10261–10270; General Mining Act of May 10, 1872, ch. 152, 17 stat. 91 (codified as amended at 30 U.S.C. §§ 21–54).

216. *Ogden Junction*, April 18, 1874; Record card, April 15, 1874, Third Judicial District Federal Court, Salt Lake City, UT; Minnesota Historical Society, "Becoming a Citizen: Naturalization Records, 1850–1930," video podcast transcript, 2012, https://www.youtube.com/watch?v=jH9xCXJwKf0; National Archives and Records Administration, "Naturalization Records," https://www.archives.gov/research/immigration/naturalization; D'Vera Cohn, "How U.S. Immigration Laws and Rules Have Changed Through History," Pew Research Center, https://www.pewresearch.org/fact-tank/2015/09/30/how-u-s-immigration-laws-and-rules-have-changed-through-history/.

217. *Sacramento Bee*, December 2, 1863; *Gold Hill Daily News*, August 1, 1864, January 13, 1865, August 8, 1865, March 23,1867; *Utah Mining Journal*, October 21, 1872, January 27, 1873; *Deseret News*, November 27, 1872; *New North-West*, July 13, 1877; *Daily Intermountain*, March 19, 1889; *New York Times*, July 22, 1902; *Intermountain Catholic*, May 30, 1908; *Los Angeles Times*, November 7, 1925; *Salt Lake Tribune*, November 7, 1925, November 10, 1925, December 31, 1925; *Idaho Statesman*, November 8, 1925; *Fowler Ensign*, November 12, 1925; Find a Grave, "Death of Mr. Colbath," undated clipping, https://www.findagrave.com/memorial/159464/lemuel-ulysses-colbath.

218. *Daily Ogden Junction*, March 15, 1875; *Salt Lake Herald-Republican*, July 15, 1875; *Salt Lake Tribune*, May 11, 1875, March 17, 1876, April 9, 1876; *San Francisco Examiner*, July 15, 1875; *Sacramento Bee*, March 15, 1876; *Los Angeles Daly Star*, March 15, 1876; *Salt Lake Herald-Republican*, June 16, 1899; *Montana Standard*, May 16, 1937.

219. Everhart, *Mining Frontier*, 43; Arthur C. Spencer, *The Atlantic Gold District and the North Laramie Mountains* (Washington, D.C.: Government Printing Office, 1916), 10, 23–24; Tullidge, *History of Salt Lake City*, 690–93; Church History Database, "Zenos Evans"; U.S. federal census, 1860 and 1870.

220. *Utah Mining Gazette*, September 6, 1873; Bliss, *Merchants and Miners*, 182–83; Marcosson, *Anaconda*, 44; Sloan, *Gazetteer of Utah*, 93.

221. *Utah Mining Gazette*, September 6, 1873, March 14, 1874.

222. Powell, *Dalys*, 7, 30, 33; Toole, "Marcus Daly," 8–9.

223. *Deseret News*, September 18, 1872; *Salt Lake Herald Republican*, November 14, 1900; *In re Daly's estate*, 36 N.Y.S.2d 954 (1942); Bernstein, *George Hearst*, 100; Marcosson, *Anaconda*, 44; Toole, "Marcus Daly," 9fn12.

224. Reilly video, 20:50–21:15; Crosserlough Parish, "Our Three Churches," http://crosserloughparish.ie/?page_id=18.

225. *Utah Weekly Miner*, January 24, 1876.

226. Emmons, *American Pale*, 270–71, 277–78.

227. Dwyer, *Story of the Cathedral*, 14–15; Reeve, "Scanlan Established Catholic Church"; Emmons, *American Pale*, 277.

228. Dwyer, *Story of the Cathedral*, 11; Reeve, "Scanlan Established Catholic Church"; *Salt Lake Tribune*, October 23, 1875; *Intermountain Catholic*, October 12, 1899; Utah Division of State History, "Salt Lake City Hospitals," https://history.utah.gov/repository-item/hospitals/; Marcus Daly Memorial Hospital, "About Us," https://www.mdmh.org/About-Us.aspx.

229. Daly, *Biography*, 5; Malone, *Battle for Butte*, 19–20.

230. *Butte Miner*, June 13, 1876, June 17, 1876, June 27, 1876; *Montana Standard*, March 31, 1985; Glasscock, *War of the Copper Kings*, loc. 634; Leeson, *History of Montana*, 953; Malone, *Battle for Butte*, 19; Rickard, *History of American Mining*, 349; Toole, "Marcus Daly," 11–12; Carter, "The Legend."

231. *Anaconda Standard*, November 1, 1895; *New North-West*, August 25, 1876; Bliss, *Merchants and Miners*, 186–87; Toole, "Marcus Daly," 13.

Chapter 6

232. Carter, "The Legend."

233. *Progressive Men*, 16; Malone, *Battle for Butte*, 18.

234. *Butte Miner*, July 22, 1876; *Anaconda Standard*, November 1, 1895; Malone, *Battle for Butte*, 19–20.

235. *New North-West*, August 25, 1876.

236. Ellen Baumler, "Montana State Fairgrounds Racetrack," National Register of Historic Places registration form, Montana State Historic Preservation Office, March 2006, 2; Dorene Courchene, ed., *Powell County: Where It All Began* (Deer Lodge, MT: Powell County Museum and Arts Foundation, 1989), 13, 102.

237. Grant, *Very Close to Trouble*, 16, 49–50; Atherton, *Cattle Kings*, 8–9.

238. *Montana Post*, November 19, 1864; Atherton, *Cattle Kings*, 88, 183–84; Crouch, *Bonanza King*, 116; Grant, *Very Close to Trouble*, 1, 4, 9–10, 38–50, 59–62, 69fn3, 83, 86–88, 134–35, 193–95; Kohrs, *Autobiography*, 43; Rosenberg, "Hard Winter," 13.

239. *Independent Record*, August 19, 1876; *New North-West*, May 27, 1870, May 9, 1874, May 25, 1883; Kohrs, *Autobiography*, 51, 72, 96; Rosenberg, "Hard Winter," 27, 50–51; John Milner Associates Inc., "Grant-Kohrs Ranch"; "Death of John Bielenberg," *Breeder's Gazette*, 47; Wahler, *Montana Horse Racing*, 47–49; Patricia Neil Warren, "John Bielenberg," Grant-Kohrs Ranch Foundation, October 29, 2014, http://www.gkrf.org/john-bielenberg/.

240. *New North-West*, July 9, 1869, July 30, 1869, August 6, 1869; Lyndel Meikle, KQRV interview notes, July 25, 2016.

241. *Butte Miner*, July 3, 1877; *New North-West*, January 31, 1874; *Independent Record*, June 2, 1874; *Helena Weekly Herald*, July 5, 1877; Kohrs, *Autobiography*, 40; Malone, *Battle for Butte*, 16–17.

242. *New North-West*, March 17, 1871, April 20, 1872, February 7, 1874; *Independent Record*, June 2, 1874; *Helena Weekly Herald*, November 21, 1872, July 17, 1873, April 1, 1875, July 5, 1877.

243. *New North-West*, April 28, 1876, August 25, 1876; *Helena Weekly Herald*, July 5, 1877; Malone, *Battle for Butte*, 16; Smith, *Reduction Plants*, 5.

244. *Helena Weekly Herald*, July 5, 1877.

245. Freeman, *Brief History*, 7–10; Malone, *Battle for Butte*, 7–8.

246. *Montana Post*, November 16, 1867; *New North-West*, October 22, 1875; Freeman, *Brief History*, 7–12; Malone, *Battle for Butte*, 8–11; Toole, "Marcus Daly," 10; Raymer, "History of Copper Mining," 21–22; Smith, *Reduction Plants*, 1–3.

247. Freeman, *Brief History*, 11–12; Malone, *Battle for Butte*, 8–11; Raymer, "History of Copper Mining," 21–22; Smith, *Reduction Plants*, 2–3; Toole, "Marcus Daly," 10; Toole, *Montana*, 157.

248. *Polk City Directory* (Butte, MT: n.p., 1884), 21–22; Malone, *Battle for Butte*, 11; Shoebotham, *Anaconda*, 37.

249. *New North-West*, October 22, 1875; Freeman, *Brief History*, 14–15; Malone, *Battle for Butte*, 15; Meade, "Fall in Price," 332; Toole, "Marcus Daly," 11–12; Writers' Project of Montana, *Copper Camp*, 297; Silver Bow County property records, see also 30 USC §§ 28b–28e and 43 CFR 3832.11.

250. *New North-West*, October 29, 1875; *Anaconda Standard*, March 27, 1921; Freeman, *Brief History*, 13–15; Malone, *Battle for Butte*, 15–17; Writers' Project of Montana, *Copper Camp*, 26–28; Armstrong correspondence, October 11, 2021.

251. Malone, *Battle for Butte*, 16.

252. *Butte Miner*, January 6, 1880.

253. O'Farrell, *Butte*, 10.

254. Dedman and Newell, *Empty Mansions*, 18–23; Howard, *Montana*, 58; William Daniel Mangam, *The Clarks, an American Phenomenon* (New York: Silver Bow Press, 1941), 7–10.

255. *Anaconda Standard*, February 28, 1908; Dedman and Newell, *Empty Mansions*, 18–23, 27–30; Freeman, *Brief History*, 39–40; Howard, *Montana*, 58; Lindsay, *Amazing Experiences*, 90; Malone, *Battle for Butte*, 12–14.

256. Phil Dougherty, "Larrabee, Charles Xavier (1843–1914)," HistoryLink.org, essay 20271, 2016, https://historylink.org/File/20271; Dedman and Newell, *Empty Mansions*, 38; Gibson, "Episode 100: Donnell, Clark and Larabie," *Verdigris*; Gibson, "Two Butte Bankers"; Glasscock, *War of the Copper Kings*, loc. 588; Malone, *Battle for Butte*, 14.

257. *New North-West*, October 18, 1878, October 17, 1879; *Sun*, February 6, 1887; *Nebraska State Journal*, April 13, 1887; *St. Louis Post-Dispatch*, November 19, 1888;

Anaconda Standard, January 1, 1922; Catharine Melin-Moser, "In the Winner's Circle," *Montana: The Magazine of Western History* vol. 64, no. 4 (Winter 2014): 29–34; Wahler, *Montana Horse Racing*, 50–51.

258. *Oregon Journal*, April 27, 1914; Dedman and Newell, *Empty Mansions*, 38–41; Freeman, *Brief History*, 40–41; Gibson, "Episode 100: Donnell, Clark and Larabie," *Verdigris*; Gibson, "Two Butte Bankers"; Glasscock, *War of the Copper Kings*, loc. 634; Malone, *Battle for Butte*, 14–15.

259. *New North-West*, October 29, 1875; Dedman and Newell, *Empty Mansions*, 38–41; Freeman, *Brief History*, 40; Malone, *Battle for Butte*, 14–15; Toole, "Marcus Daly," 23.

260. *Helena Weekly Herald*, June 8, 1876, January 1, 1880; Freeman, *Brief History*, 40; Glasscock, *War of the Copper Kings*, loc. 600; Richard I. Gibson, "The Early Mills of Butte Had Plenty of Work," *Montana Standard*, October 4, 2021; Malone, *Battle for Butte*, 16–17; Silver Bow County property records, 1877.

261. Richard I. Gibson, "Butte-Argenta Copper Co. Tried to Make a Go of Old Mining Site in the Pioneers," *Montana Standard*, October 17, 2016; Richard I. Gibson, "Cast Iron Helped Build Butte," *Montana Standard*, October 23, 2017; Samuel T. Hauser, letter, November 28, 1889, Samuel T. Hauser papers, Montana Historical Society Archives, sec. 37, box 7; Malone, *Battle for Butte*, 11–12, 19; Charles White Merrill, *Summarized Data of Silver Production* (Washington, D.C.: Bureau of Mines, U.S. Department of Commerce, 1930), 19; Robbins, "Deconstruction," 20–33; Toole, "Marcus Daly," 57.

262. Toole, "Marcus Daly," 28.

263. *New North-West*, October 29, 1875.

264. *Owyhee Bullion*, February 7, 1867; *New North-West*, November 5, 1875, December 3, 1875, December 17, 1875; Gibson, "Walkerville"; Gibson, "Rolla Butcher"; Weed, "Geology and Ore Deposits," 19, 244; U.S. federal census, 1870, Corinne, UT; Silver Bow County property records (Butcher's January 2 claim location was filed on January 12, 1875).

265. *New North-West*, October 29, 1875; Gibson, "Walkerville"; Gibson, "Rolla Butcher"; Silver Bow County property records.

266. *New North-West*, April 2, 1875, October 22, 1875, December 3, 1875, December 17, 1875, January 14, 1876; assorted advertisements, *Butte Miner*, June 10, 1876; Freeman, *Brief History*, 10; Smith, *Reduction Plants*, 2–3; Writers' Project of Montana, *Copper Camp*, 16, 26; Silver Bow County property records.

267. *Butte Miner*, June 13, 1876, June 17, 1876, June 27, 1876

268. *Butte Miner*, July 22, 1876; *Helena Weekly Herald*, October 5, 1876; *Salt Lake Herald*, December 23, 1880; Glasscock, *War of the Copper Kings*, loc. 692; Toole, "Marcus Daly," 13.

269. *New North-West*, September 29, 1876, October 13, 1876; *Salt Lake Tribune*, October 1, 1876; *Butte Miner*, October 3, 1876; *Helena Weekly Herald*, October 5, 1876; "Joseph R. Walker" purchases, Silver Bow County property records.

270. *Butte Miner*, October 3, 1876; Bliss, *Merchants and Miners*, 187–89; Silver Bow County property records.

271. *New North-West*, September 29, 1876, October 13, 1876; *Butte Miner*, October 10, 1876, October 31, 1876, December 12, 1876, January 9, 1877; *Anaconda Standard*, November 1, 1895; Bliss, *Merchants and Miners*, 187–89; Glasscock, *War of the Copper Kings*, loc. 726; Malone, *Battle for Butte*, 20; *New World Encyclopedia*, "Marcus Daly," https://www.newworldencyclopedia.org; Silver Bow County property records.

272. Emmons, *Butte Irish*, 99–102; Toole, "Marcus Daly," 24, 57–62; Toole, "Genesis," 21, 26–28.

273. B.E. Stack, "Origin of the Clark-Daly Feud," (1933) unsigned typescript, "Marcus Daly," vertical file, MHS; Toole, "Genesis," 26–27; Senate testimony 1900, 2205.

274. Connolly, "Story of Montana," 85; Howard, *Montana*, 59; Lindsay, *Amazing Experiences*, 85; Malone, *Battle for Butte*, 17–18.

275. Malone, *Battle for Butte*, 12–15; Place, *Copper Kings*, 35; Toole, "Marcus Daly," 17–19, 23; Connolly, "Story of Montana," 94; Robbins, "Deconstruction," 31.

276. Emmons, "The Orange and the Green"; Foster, *Modern Ireland*, 214.

277. *Butte Miner*, April 23, 1878; Toole, "Genesis," 24–25.

278. *New North-West*, February 2, 1877, February 9, 1877; *Montana Standard*, July 15, 1941; U.S. federal census, 1880, Butte City, MT; Silver Bow County property records.

279. *Utah Mining Gazette*, March 14, 1874; *New North-West*, March 9, 1877; *Butte Miner*, April 23, 1878, December 2, 1879, April 20, 1880, September 3, 1880; *Anaconda Standard*, June 3, 1900, January 28, 1903; Freeman, *Brief History*, 16; Toole, "Marcus Daly," 16; U.S. federal census, 1880, Butte City, Montana Territory.

280. *Utah Mining Gazette*, February 14, 1874; *Butte Miner*, April 17, 1877, April 30, 1881; *Independent Record*, June 23, 1877; *New North-West*, October 26, 1877; Bliss, *Merchants and Miners*, 188–90; Leeson, *History of Montana*, 953.

281. Bliss, *Merchants and Miners*, 190–91; Glasscock, *War of the Copper Kings*, loc. 703.

282. *Independent Record*, May 8, 1877; *Butte Miner*, January 8, 1878; Gibson, "Walkerville."

283. *New North-West*, August 10, 1877.

284. Kristen Inbody, "Big Hole Battle Continues to Resonate 140 Years Later," *Great Falls Tribune*, August 1, 2017.

285. *New North-West*, August 17, 1877, August 28, 1877; *Butte Miner*, May 8, 1880; National Park Service, "Montana: Big Hole National Battlefield," U.S. Department of the Interior, https://www.nps.gov/articles/bighole.htm; Powell, *Dalys*, 8; Shoebotham, *Anaconda*, 42; Toole, "Marcus Daly," 24–25.

286. *Independent Record*, March 24, 1878.

287. Bliss, *Merchants and Miners*, 200.

288. Calvert, *Gibraltar*, 5; Emmons, *Butte Irish*, 225–26.

289. *Butte Miner*, June 18, 1878, June 25, 1878; Paddy Dennehy, "Miner's Union Day Dates from 1878," *Montana Standard*, June 12, 2018; Gibson, "Episode 115: Butte in 1878," *Verdigris*; Malone, *Battle for Butte*, 76; Rickard, *History of American Mining*, 349; Toole, "History of the Anaconda," 157–58.

290. *Butte Miner*, November 4, 1879, December 9, 1879; *Anaconda Standard*, November 18, 1923; Freeman, *Brief History*, 17; Gibson, "Episode 216: Williamsburg," *Verdigris*; Raymer, "History of Copper Mining," 20–22; Kirchoff, "Copper Industry," 336–38; Rickard, *History of American Mining*, 350–55; Quivic, "Smoke and Tailings," 113; Smith, *Reduction Plants*, 5–7; Weed, "Geology and Ore Deposits," 20.

291. *New North-West*, March 28, 1879; *Butte Miner*, June 10, 1879, August 19, 1879, August 26, 1879; *Anaconda Standard*, October 6, 1895, November 1, 1895; Silver Bow County property records.

292. *Independent Record*, March 24, 1878; Samuel T. Hauser, letter, March 28, 1878, Samuel T. Hauser papers, MHS; Toole, "Marcus Daly," 27; Toole, "History of the Anaconda," 13, 16.

293. Leeson, *History of Montana*, 953; Shoebotham, *Anaconda*, 49.

294. *Butte Miner*, January 6, 1880; *Salt Lake Tribune*, May 8, 1910; Bliss, *Merchants and Miners*, 194–95; Alice Gold and Silver Mining Company (F000018), Montana Secretary of State, April 2, 1880, filed March 17, 1880; see also *Geddes v. Anaconda Copper Mining Company*, 254 U.S. 590 (1921).

295. *New North-West*, June 20, 1879.

296. *Butte Miner*, March 13, 1877; Emmons, *Butte Irish*, 21; Toole, "Marcus Daly," 16.

297. *Independent Record*, July 31, 1879; *Butte Miner*, March 27, 1877, February 19, 1878, August 31, 1879, October 7, 1879; *Helena Weekly Herald*, January 1, 1880; Butte Catholic Community North, "St. Patrick Church," www.butteccn.org; U.S. federal census, 1880, Butte City, Montana Territory.

298. *Montana Post*, July 17, 1868; J.H. Ostberg, *Sketches of Old Butte* (N.p.: self-published booklet, 1972), 29; VF1228.1, Butte Silver Bow Public Archives; Wahler, *Montana Horse Racing*, 67, 112, 123.

299. *Butte Miner*, June 12, 1877; *New North-West*, March 12, 1875, November 5, 1875, June 1, 1877.

300. *Butte Miner*, February 5, 1878, August 20, 1878, July 13, 1880; *New North-West*, September 6, 1878, October 18, 1878; *Independent Record*, August 19, 1876; Richard I. Gibson, "Horse, Greyhound Racing Have Rich History in Butte," *Montana Standard*, July 4, 2016; John Milner Associates Inc., "Grant-Kohrs Ranch"; "Death of John Bielenberg," *Breeder's Gazette*, 47; Kohrs, *Conrad Kohrs*, 72; Wahler, *Montana Horse Racing*, 80–86.

301. Charlie Larson, "Mayors of Butte," VF 1158, BSB.

302. *Montana Post*, November 16, 1867; *Butte Miner*, September 10, 1878, August 19, 1879; Freeman, *Brief History*, 12; Gibson, "Episode 92: John Noyes,"

Verdigris; Glasscock, *War of the Copper Kings*, loc. 576; Lindsay, *Amazing Experiences*, 12, 18, 22; Malone, *Battle for Butte*, 8; *Progressive Men*, 488–89; Shoebotham, *Anaconda*, 49–50; Toole, "Marcus Daly," 29; "Noyes, John," vertical file, BSB.

303. *Butte Miner*, July 13, 1880; *New North-West*, August 26, 1881; "Butte Track Twenty Years Old," *Daily Racing Form*, July 3, 1907; Janet Charlene Thomson, "Role of Lee Mantle in Montana Politics, 1889–1900: An Interpretation," master's thesis, University of Montana, 1956, 2–9; Silver Bow County property records.

304. *Butte Miner*, June 10, 1879, June 24, 1879, April 28, 1886, June 23, 1886, August 11, 1886; *Independent Record*, July 31, 1879, May 14, 1886; *River Press*, June 23, 1886; West Side Fair and Racing Association (D000438), 1886, Domestic Profit Corporation, Montana Secretary of State.

305. *Butte Miner*, July 15, 1879, August 31, 1879, September 2, 1879, September 9, 1879; Glasscock, *War of the Copper Kings*, loc. 1,900.

Chapter 7

306. *Anaconda Standard*, October 6, 1895; *Fergus County Argus*, October 31, 1895 (reprint from *New York Tribune*); Brown, "Ore Deposits of Butte City," 555–56; Lindsay, *Amazing Experiences*, 16–17, 91.

307. *Anaconda Standard*, January 29, 1909; Malone, *Battle for Butte*, 24–25; Toole, "Marcus Daly," 30; Silver Bow County property records.

308. *Butte Miner*, August 19, 1879; *Anaconda Standard*, October 6, 1895, November 1, 1895.

309. *Anaconda Standard*, October 6, 1895, November 1, 1895; Lindsay, *Amazing Experiences*, 93–98.

310. *Anaconda Standard*, October 6, 1895, November 1, 1895; Toole, "Marcus Daly," 27–28; Toole, "History of the Anaconda," 13, 16; Silver Bow County property records.

311. *Butte Miner*, July 22, 1880; *Butte Miner*, August 17, 1880; *Butte Miner*, October 16, 1880; *Butte Miner*, October 27, 1880; Silver Bow County property records.

312. *New North-West*, October 18, 1878; *Butte Miner*, March 9, 1880, November 2, 1880, December 7, 1880, May 3, 1881; *Madisonian*, August 14, 1880, October 12, 1911; *Anaconda Standard*, January 25, 1924; LOC, "About the *Weekly Miner* (Butte, Mont.) 1878–1881," https://www.loc.gov/item/sn84036032/; Swibold, *Copper Chorus*, 9, 24. John Read was at the *Miner* by 1877, later joining Lee Mantle's team as city editor of the *Butte Inter-Mountain*.

313. *Anaconda Standard*, November 1, 1895; *Daily Evening Herald*, November 20, 1865; *Helena Weekly Herald*, January 1, 1880; *Helena Weekly Herald*, June 2, 1881; Freeman, *Brief History*, 2, 17; Gibson, "Episode 191: Montana Copper Company," *Verdigris*; Malone, *Battle for Butte*, 61.

314. *Butte Miner*, January 6, 1880; Bliss, *Merchants and Miners*, 197; Marcosson, *Anaconda*, 45.

315. *Butte Miner*, May 7, 1880, May 11, 1880; *Anaconda Standard*, November 1, 1895; Bliss, *Merchants and Miners*, 198; Quivic, "Smoke and Tailings," 144; Shoebotham, *Anaconda*, 49; Silver Bow County property records. Lindsay, *Amazing Experiences* gives the $100,000 figure on page 67 but gives the $30,000–$100,000 range on page 96.

316. *Butte Miner*, June 26, 1880; *Helena Weekly Herald*, January 1, 1880, April 8, 1880; *New York Tribune*, August 16, 1880; *Salt Lake Herald*, December 23, 1880; Silver Bow County property records.

317. Bliss, *Merchants and Miners*, 197; Quivic, "Smoke and Tailings," 155; James and Fell, "Alta," 280.

318. *Anaconda Standard*, November 1, 1895; Bliss, *Merchants and Miners*, 197; Lindsay, *Amazing Experiences*, 96; Malone, *Battle for Butte*, 25; Quivic, "Smoke and Tailings," 155.

319. *Butte Miner*, May 14, 1882; *Black Hills Union*, June 23, 1899; Gibson, "Two Butte Bankers"; Gibson, "R.C. Chambers"; Lindsay, *Amazing Experiences*, 93–94; Toole, "Marcus Daly," 31; Silver Bow County property records.

320. *Salt Lake Herald-Republican*, November 14, 1900; Malone, *Battle for Butte*, 27–28; Toole, "Marcus Daly," 27–28.

321. *Butte Miner*, May 13, 1880, May 26, 1880; Crouch, *Bonanza King*, 380; U.S. federal census, 1880, Storey County, NV.

322. *Butte Miner*, July 26, 1880, August 10, 1880, August 17, 1880, August 19, 1880; *San Francisco Examiner*, July 28, 1880.

323. *New North-West*, April 23, 1880; *Salt Lake Herald*, July 12, 1881; *Montana Standard*, August 22, 1943; Connolly, *Devil Learns*, 86–87; Lindsay, *Amazing Experiences*, 67, 70, 74; Malone, *Battle for Butte*, 24–25.

324. Powell, *Dalys*, 8; Toole, "Marcus Daly," 29. Toole's 1948 account is the earliest version of the "laundry story" found to date, and his source is an oral history given to him by Mrs. T.J. Murray.

325. *Butte Miner*, October 10, 1880, December 5, 1880.

326. *New North-West*, May 7, 1880; *Madisonian*, February 5, 1881; Central Pacific Railroad Photographic History Museum, "Central Pacific and Union Pacific Railroad Timetables, May 1, 1882," 2014, http://cprr.org/Museum/Ephemera/CP-UP_Timetable_1882.html; Wrigley, "Utah and Northern Railway," 245–53.

327. *Butte Miner*, January 18, 1881, January 22, 1881; *Anaconda Standard*, November 13, 1900; Lindsay, *Amazing Experiences*, 82, 97–98; Tracy Thornton, "St. Patrick's Cemetery Angel a Symbol of Resilience," *Montana Standard*, September 13, 2020.

328. *Daily Deadwood Pioneer-Times*, June 22, 1878; *Butte Miner*, August 25, 1881; Malone, *Battle for Butte*, 26–27; Nasaw, *Chief*, 23–24; Smith, "Here's to Low-Grade Ore," 10–14; Toole, "Marcus Daly," 27.

329. *Weekly Mercury*, January 28, 1881; Harrison, *Progressive Americans*, 147; Igler, *Industrial Cowboys*, 101–3; Phelps, *California's Representative Men*, 325; Sergent, "Pastime of Millions," 55–60, 74, 98–100, 117.

330. *Butte Miner*, January 18, 1881; Lindsay, *Amazing Experiences*, 98–99; Silver Bow County property records.

331. *Independent Record*, March 27, 1881; *Butte Miner*, January 25, 1881, April 5, 1881, May 3, 1881.

332. *Butte Miner*, May 31, 1881; *Independent Record*, June 2, 1881; *Montana Standard*, July 21, 1950; Lindsay, *Amazing Experiences*, 91; Malone, *Battle for Butte*, 27–28, Toole, "History of the Anaconda," 18; Silver Bow County property records.

333. *Montana Standard*, July 21, 1950; Gibson, "Episode 275: Anaconda Company Heritage," *Verdigris*; Malone, *Battle for Butte*, 27–28, 204; Toole, "Marcus Daly," 2–33, 158–59, 177; Toole, "History of the Anaconda," 18.

334. *Butte Miner*, August 6, 1881; Silver Bow County property records.

335. *Butte Miner*, June 22, 1881, July 16, 1881; *Salt Lake Herald*, July 12, 1881; Goodwin, "Marcus Daly," 271; Archival guide, Charles Carroll Goodwin Papers, University of Nevada, Reno, https://archive.library.unr.edu/public/repositories/2/resources/16.

336. *Butte Miner*, July 16, 1881, September 1, 1881, January 1, 1882.

337. *Butte Miner*, July 3, 1881, July 28, 1881; *Independent Record*, September 3, 1881; Lindsay, *Amazing Experiences*, 98; LOC, "About *Daily Miner*," https://chroniclingamerica.loc.gov/lccn/sn85053057/.

338. *Independent Record*, September 3, 1881; *Helena Weekly Herald*, November 3, 1881; *Butte Miner*, June 2, 1881, May 23, 1882, July 2, 1882; *Anaconda Standard*, November 13, 1900; Malone, *Battle for Butte*, 27–28.

339. Phil Connelly, "The Grand Old Opera House," *Ravalli Republic*, October 7, 2017; Gregory Llewellyn Gordon, "Money Does Grow on Trees: A.B. Hammond and the Age of the Lumber Baron," master's thesis, University of Montana, 166, 171, 235; Mawdsley, "Square Set Method," 1070–1074.

Chapter 8

340. Lindsay, *Amazing Experiences*, 21.

341. *Butte Miner*, November 18, 1880, November 24, 1880; Lindsay, *Amazing Experiences*, 20–21.

342. Horace Pops, "Processing of Wire from Antiquity to the Future," *Wire Journal International*, June 2008, 60–66.

343. *Montana Post*, November 16, 1867; *Montana Standard*, July 13, 1961; Brown, "Ore Deposits of Butte City," 554–58; Hoffman correspondence, July 20, 2022; Kirchoff, "Copper Industry," 340; Lindsay, *Amazing Experiences*, 98; Mawdsley, "Square Set Method," 1,069; Marcosson, *Anaconda*, 26; O'Farrell, *Butte*, 28; *Ores and Metals*, 175, 236, 242; A.B. Parson, ed., *Seventy-Five Years of Progress in the Mineral Industry 1871–1946* (N.p.: American Institute of Mining, 1947), 128, 137, 209; Raymer, "History of Copper Mining," 14; Rickard, *History of American Mining*, 346–50; Smith, *Reduction Plants*, 10–11; Libor Vejmelek and Scott B. Smithson, "Seismic Reflection Profiling in the Boulder Batholith, Montana," *Geology* 20, no. 9 (September 1995): 811; Weed, "Geology and Ore Deposits," 20; World Museum of Mining displays, Butte, MT, March 22, 2022.

344. Brown, "Ore Deposits of Butte City," 554–58; Kirchoff, "Copper Industry," 340; Lindsay, *Amazing Experiences*, 98; Mawdsley, "Square Set Method," 1,069; Marcosson, *Anaconda*, 26; Raymer, "History of Copper Mining," 14; Rickard, *History of American Mining*, 346; Smith, *Reduction Plants*, 10–11; Weed, "Geology and Ore Deposits," 20. In 1884, ore diluted with low-grade wall rock averaged 12 to 14 percent copper per ton. The last ore mined from the Berkeley pit was 0.61 percent copper. Remaining vein mines underground were estimated at 4 percent. The 2021 estimates at Butte's Continental pit are approximately 0.35 percent copper. *See* Hoffman correspondence, July 20, 2022; Keith R. Long, "Reserves and Production Data for Selected Ore Deposits in the United States Found in the Files of the Anaconda Copper Company," open-file report 92-002, U.S. Department of the Interior, U.S. Geological Survey, 1992, 9–10.

345. National Park Service, "Timeline of Michigan Copper Mining Prehistory to 1850," Keweenaw National Historic Park, https://www.nps.gov/kewe/learn/historyculture/copper-mining-timeline.htm; David Malakoff, "Ancient Native Americans Were Among the World's First Coppersmiths," *Science*, March 19, 2021; Rickard, *History of American Mining*, 231; Horace J. Stevens, *The Copper Handbook*, vol. 8 (Houghton, MI: Horace Stevens, 1909), 1,466; Toole, "History of the Anaconda," 26–28.

346. Rickard, *History of American Mining*, 278; Toole, "History of the Anaconda," 21–28.

347. *Anaconda Standard*, November 18, 1923; Kirchoff, "Copper Industry," 336–38; Quivic, "Smoke and Tailings," 113; Raymer, "History of Copper Mining," 20–21; Rickard, *History of American Mining*, 350–55; Smith, *Reduction Plants*, 1–2; Weed, "Geology and Ore Deposits," 20.

348. *Montana Post*, July 31, 1868; *Helena Weekly Herald*, February 1, 1872; Lindsay, *Amazing Experiences*, 90; Raymer, "History of Copper Mining," 26; Rickard, *History of American Mining*, 278, 347–54; Weed, "Geology and Ore Deposits," 20.

349. Gibson, "Episode 185: Butte Reduction Works," *Verdigris*; Richard I. Gibson, *Montana Standard*, May 6, 2019; Lindsay, *Amazing Experiences*, 101; MacMillan,

Smoke Wars, 8, 262; Quivic, "Smoke and Tailings," 146; Smith, *Reduction Plants*, 2–3, 6.

350. *River Press*, January 19, 1881; *New North-West*, February 4, 1881; *Butte Miner*, February 8, 1881, February 17, 1881; *Helena Weekly Herald*, February 24, 1881; U.S. federal census, 1880, Butte City, Montana Territory.

351. *Butte Miner*, February 17, 1881.

352. Rickard, *History of American Mining*, 350; Wrigley, "Utah and Northern Railway," 245–53.

353. Wrigley, "Utah and Northern Railway," 245–53.

354. *Daily Ogden Junction*, January 9, 1879; Utah Rails, "Utah and Northern Railway," http://utahrails.net/utahrails/utah-and-northern-ry-1878-1889.php; Wrigley, "Utah and Northern Railway," 245–53.

355. *Butte Miner*, September 9, 1879.

356. *Butte Miner*, April 3, 1880.

357. *River Press*, November 2, 1881; *New North-West*, December 23, 1881; Richard I. Gibson, "Butte's First Railroad was Clandestine," *Montana Standard*, August 26, 2019; Richard I. Gibson, "Melrose Had Raucous Beginnings," *Montana Standard*, January 17, 2022.

358. *Butte Miner*, September 2, 1907.

359. *Butte Miner*, January 27, 1882, February 5, 1882.

360. *Butte Miner*, February 7, 1882 (reprinting, *Salt Lake Tribune*, February 4, 1882); *Butte Miner*, May 21, 1882, May 24, 1882, June 1, 1882.

361. *Butte Miner*, June 11, 1882.

362. *Butte Miner*, June 2, 1882.

363. *Butte Miner*, June 9, 1882, June 10, 1882.

364. *Butte Miner*, June 24, 1882.

365. *Los Angeles Herald*, May 18, 1882; *Stockton Daily Evening Mail*, June 20, 1882; *Daily Bee*, June 23, 1882; *Oakland Tribune*, June 29, 1882; Bernstein, *George Hearst*, 141–45.

366. Bernstein, *George Hearst*, 140–41; Lindsay, *Amazing Experiences*, 75, 94–95; Toole, "History of the Anaconda," 18, 22–23.

367. Lindsay, *Amazing Experiences*, 75, 94–95; Nickliss, *Phoebe Apperson Hearst*, 66–68; Toole, "History of the Anaconda," 18, 22–23.

368. Goodwin, "Marcus Daly," 271; Lindsay, *Amazing Experiences*, 94–95; Toole, "History of the Anaconda," 22–23. The *Anaconda Standard*, on November 18, 1923, attributed the story to Harry Gallwey, another Comstock veteran. A similar version was published in the *Anaconda Standard* on July 2, 1922.

369. *Butte Miner*, August 5, 1882, August 6, 1882, August 27, 1882, September 2, 1882; Anaconda Copper Mining Company, *Copper: From Mine to Finished Product* (New York: United Metals Selling Company, 1920), 8.

370. *Anaconda Standard*, November 14, 1900.

371. *Butte Miner*, October 21, 1882, quoting *Salt Lake Tribune*, September 17, 1882.

372. *Butte Miner*, November 18, 1882.

373. Pit Watch, "Berkeley Pit Superfund," https://pitwatch.org/superfund/.

374. Gibson, "Nature-Built Landscape," 5.

375. *Butte Miner*, April 28, 1886; *Daily Inter-Mountain*, September 24, 1886; *Anaconda Standard*, June 19, 1892, October 5, 1893; *New York Times*, September 28, 1893; "Montana's Greatest Turfman," *Daily Racing Form*, December 22, 1912; *Montana Standard*, March 29, 1929; Connolly, *Devil Learns*, 90–91; Historical Company, *American Turf*, 178–209.

SELECTED BIBLIOGRAPHY

Full citations of sources used only once in the text can be found in the endnotes (they are not listed here). Web links were accessed live on August 1, 2022, unless otherwise noted. Many print sources are also accessible online.

Adelman, Melvin L. "The First Modern Sport in America: Harness Racing in New York City, 1825–1870." *Journal of Sport History* 8, no. 1 (1981): 5–32.

Archives West. "Walker Brothers Papers, 1860–1895." Historical Note. http://archiveswest.orbiscascade.org/ark:/80444/xv59246.

Armstrong, David. Interview, March 22, 2022, email correspondence, December 2021–August 2022.

Atherton, Lewis. *The Cattle Kings*. Lincoln: University of Nebraska Press, 1972.

Beretta, Patrick. Interview, March 22, 2022, email correspondence, November 19, 2021–July 13, 2022.

Bernstein, Matthew. *George Hearst: Silver King of the Gilded Age*. Norman: University of Oklahoma Press, 2021.

Bethel, A.C.W. "The Golden Skein: California's Gold-Rush Transportation Network." In *A Golden State: Mining and Economic Development in Gold Rush California*. Berkeley: University of California Press, 1999.

Bliss, Jonathan. *Merchants and Miners in Utah: The Walker Brothers and their Bank*. Salt Lake City, UT: Western Epics, 1983.

Breeder's Gazette. "Death of John Bielenberg." July 13, 1922, 47.

Brewer, William H., and Francis Peloubet Farquhar. *Up and Down California in 1860–1864: The Journal of William H. Brewer*. 2nd ed. Berkeley: University of California Press, 1949.

Brown, R.G. "The Ore Deposits of Butte City." *Transactions of the American Institute of Mining and Metallurgical Engineering* 24 (1894): 543–58.

Calvert, Jerry W. *The Gibraltar: Socialism and Labor in Butte, Montana, 1895–1920.* Helena: Montana Historical Society Press, 1988.

Campbell, Eugene E. "Review of E.B. Long, 'The Saints and the Union: Utah Territory During the Civil War.'" *BYU Studies Quarterly* 22, no. 4 (1982): 500.

Carlisle, Rodney P. "Hearst, George." In *American National Biography*. New York: Oxford University Press, 2020. https://doi.org/10.1093/anb/9780198606697. article.0500334.

Carter, Dan. "The Legend: Two Colorful Versions." *Montana Standard*, March 31, 1985.

Church of Jesus Christ of Latter-day Saints. "Church History Biographical Database." https://history.churchofjesuschrist.org/chd/landing. (Cited as "Church History Database.")

Clayton, Lawrence, James F. Hoy, and Jerald Underwood. *Vaqueros, Cowboys, and Buckaroos: The Genesis and Life of the Mounted North American Cattle Herders.* Austin: University of Texas Press, 2001.

Colton, Walter. *Three Years in California*. New York: A.S. Barnes & Co., 1850.

Connolly, C.P. *The Devil Learns to Vote.* New York: Covici, Friede, 1938.

———. "The Story of Montana II." *McClure's Magazine* 27, no. 5 (1906): 451–65.

Cowdrey, Mike, Ned Martin, and Jody Martin. *Horses & Bridles of the American Indians.* Nicasio, CA: Hawk Hill Press, 2012.

Crouch, Gregory. *The Bonanza King: John Mackay and the Battle over the Greatest Riches in the American West.* New York: Simon and Schuster, 2019. Kindle version.

———. "The Mining Millionaire Americans Couldn't Help but Love." *Smithsonian Magazine*, June 6, 2018.

Cummings, Richard Osborne. *The American and His Food.* Chicago: University of Chicago Press, 1940. http://www.foodtimeline.org/cummings.pdf.

Cusack, Mary Frances. *Illustrated History of Ireland.* Kenmare, IE: Irish National Publications, 1875.

Daly, Hugh. *Biography of Marcus Daly of Montana.* Butte, MT: Hugh Daly, 1935.

Dedman, Bill, and Paul Clark Newell Jr. *Empty Mansions.* New York: Ballantine Books, 2013.

Dunne, Tony. Email correspondence, December 8, 2021–July 23, 2022.

Dwyer, Robert J. *The Story of the Cathedral of the Madeline 1866–1936.* Consecration souvenir booklet. Salt Lake City, UT: n.p., 1936.

Egan, Timothy. *The Immortal Irishman.* Boston: Mariner Books, 2016. Kindle edition.

Emmons, David M. *Beyond the American Pale: The Irish in the West, 1845–1910.* Norman: University of Oklahoma Press, 2011.

———. *The Butte Irish: Class and Ethnicity in an American Mining Town, 1875–1925.* Champaign: University of Illinois Press, 1989.

———. Email correspondence, April 15, 2020–September 25, 2021.

———. "The Orange and the Green in Montana: A Reconsideration of the Clark-Daly Feud." In *Montana Heritage*. Helena: Montana Historical Society Press, 1992.

Everhart, William C., ed. *The Mining Frontier*. Washington, D.C.: National Survey of Historic Sites and Buildings, United States Department of the Interior, National Park Service, 1959.

Feehan, John. *Farming in Ireland: History, Heritage and Environment*. Dublin, IE: University College Dublin, Faculty of Agriculture, 2003.

Foster, R.F. *Modern Ireland, 1600–1972*. London: Penguin Books, 1988.

Freeman, Harry C. *A Brief History of Butte, Montana*. Chicago: Henry O. Shepard Co., 1900.

Gibson, Richard I. "The Nature-Built Landscape: Geological Underpinnings of Butte." Vernacular Architecture Forum thirtieth annual meeting. Butte, MT. 2009.

———. "R.C. Chambers." *Montana Standard*, April 24, 2022.

———. "Rolla Butcher's Interesting Life and Legacy." *Montana Standard*, February 4, 2019.

———. "Two Less Well-Known Butte Bankers Who Made Their Mark." *Montana Standard*, January 16, 2017.

———. *Verdigris Project*. Podcast transcripts. 2018–2022. https://www.verdigrisproject.org/butte-americas-story.

———. "Walkerville Almost Could Have Been Rainbeau." *Montana Standard*, January 1, 2018.

Gillis, William Robert. *Gold Rush Days with Mark Twain*. New York: Albert & Charles Boni, 1930.

Glasscock, C.B. *The War of the Copper Kings*. New York: Grosset & Dunlap, 1935. Reprint, Helena, MT: Riverbend Publishing, 2002. Kindle edition.

Golway, Terry. *Machine Made: Tammany Hall and the Creation of Modern American Politics*. New York: W.W. Norton, 2014. Kindle edition.

Goodwin, C.C. "Marcus Daly." *Goodwin's Weekly*, January 27, 1912. Reprint in *As I Remember Them*. Salt Lake City, UT: Salt Lake Commercial Club, 1913.

Grant, Johnny. *Very Close to Trouble: The Johnny Grant Memoir*. Edited with historical annotations by Lyndel Meikle. Pullman: Washington State University Press, 1996.

Greene, Ann Norton. *Horses at Work: Harnessing Power in Industrial America*. Cambridge, MA: Harvard University Press, 2008.

Griffin, Brian. "The More Sport the Merrier, Say We: Sport in Ireland during the Great Famine." *Irish Economic and Social History* 45, no. 1 (December 2018): 90–114.

Griffith, Richard. *Griffith's Land Valuation* (1856–1857) Crosserlough Parish, Cavan. Accessed via https://www.askaboutireland.ie/griffith-valuation/.

Harrison, Mitchell C. *Prominent and Progressive Americans*. Vol. 1. New York: New York Tribune, 1902.

Historical Company. *The American Turf*. New York: Nicoll and Roy, 1898.

Hittell, John S. *Hittell on Gold Mines and Mining*. Quebec: G. & G.E. Desbarats, 1864. Project Gutenberg eBook, #29926.

Hoffman, Larry. Interview, March 22, 2022, email correspondence, December 2021–August 2022.

Howard, Joseph Kinsey. *Montana: High Wide and Handsome*. Lincoln: University of Nebraska Press, 1943. Reprint, 2003.

Igler, David. *Industrial Cowboys: Miller & Lux and the Transformation of the Far West, 1850–1920*. Berkeley: University of California Press, 2001.

In the Matter of the Estate of Marcus Daly. Cause no. 371. Montana Third Judicial District Court, Deer Lodge County (1901). (Cited as Daly Probate, 1901.)

James, Lawrence P., and James Fell. "Alta, the Cottonwoods and American Fork." In *From the Ground Up: The History of Mining in Utah*. Logan: Utah State University Press, 2006.

John Milner Associates Inc. "Grant-Kohrs Ranch Cultural Landscape Report, Part 1." National Park Service. July 2004.

Jung, Maureen A. "Capitalism Comes to the Diggings." *California History* 77, no. 4 (1998): 52–77.

Keeneland Racing Association Library and the University of Kentucky. *Daily Racing Form* Historical Online Archive. https://drf.uky.edu.

Kirchoff, Charles, Jr. "Copper Industry of the U.S." in *Mineral Resources of the United States, 1883–1884*. Washington: Bureau of Mines, 1885.

Kohrs, Conrad. *Conrad Kohrs: An Autobiography*. Edited by Conrad Kohrs Warren. Deer Lodge, MT: Platen Press, 1977.

Leeson, M.A. *History of Montana, 1739–1885*. Chicago: Warner, Beers & Company, 1885.

Lewis, Samuel. *Topographical Dictionary of Ireland*. London: S. Lewis and Company, 1837. https://www.libraryireland.com/topog/placeindex.php.

Library of Congress. *California as I Saw It: First-Person Narratives of California's Early Years, 1849 to 1900*. https://www.loc.gov/collections/california-first-person-narratives/articles-and-essays/early-california-history/.

Lindsay, John. *Amazing Experiences of a Judge: With an Autobiography and Tribute to Marcus Daly*. Philadelphia: Dorrance and Company, 1939.

Loomis, Noel M. *Wells Fargo: An Illustrated History*. New York: Bramhall House, 1968.

Lunsford, Sarah. "Take a Chance on a Longshot." *Calaveras Enterprise*, January 21, 2010.

Mac Cana, Proinsias. "Celtic Religion: An Overview." In *Encyclopedia of Religion*. 2nd ed. Edited by Lindsay Jones. Detroit: Macmillan Reference, 1987. Reprint, 2005.

———. "The Goddesses of the Insular Celts." In *Celtic Mythology*. London: Hamlyn, 1970. http://www.ricorso.net/rx/library/criticism/classic/Celtiana/M-Cana_P/Celtic_Myth/3_Goddess.htm

MacLeod, Sharon Paice. *Celtic Myth and Religion: A Study of Traditional Belief, with Newly Translated Prayers, Poems and Songs*. Jefferson, NC: McFarland, 2011.

MacMillan, Donald. *Smoke Wars*. Helena: Montana Historical Society Press, 2000.

Madsen, Brigham D. "General Patrick Edward Connor: Father of Utah Mining." In *From the Ground Up: The History of Mining in Utah*. Logan: Utah State University Press, 2006.

Malone, Michael P. *The Battle for Butte*. Seattle: University of Washington Press, 1981.

Marcosson, Isaac F. *Anaconda*. New York: Dodd, Meade & Company, 1957.

Markosian, Richard. "The Walker Brothers Part I—Pioneer Success Story." *Utah Stories*, November 9, 2015. https://utahstories.com/2015/11/the-walker-brothers-part-1/. (Cited as Markosian, Part I.)

———. "The Walker Brothers Part II—Camp Floyd and Beyond." *Utah Stories*, November 9, 2015. https://utahstories.com/2015/11/the-walker-brothers-part-ii/. (Cited as Markosian, Part II.)

Marshall, Howard W. "Vaqueros." *In Buckaroos in Paradise: Cowboy Life in Northern Nevada*. Reprinted 1980. https://www.loc.gov/collections/ranching-culture-in-northern-nevada-from-1945-to-1982/articles-and-essays/buckaroo-views-of-a-western-way-of-life/vaquero.

Mawdsley, J.B. "The Square Set Method of Stoping at Butte." *CIM Bulletin*, 1925.

McShane, Clay, and Joel Tarr. *The Horse in the City: Living Machines in the 19th Century*. Baltimore, MD: Johns Hopkins University Press, 2007.

Meade, Edward S. "The Fall in the Price of Silver Since 1873." *Journal of Political Economy* 5, no. 3 (June 1897): 316–39.

Miller, Kerby A. *Emigrants and Exiles, Ireland and the Irish Exodus to North America*. Oxford, UK: Oxford University Press, 1988.

Mitchel, John, et al. *The History of Ireland, Ancient and Modern*. New York: P.J. Kenedy, 1903.

Montgomery, E.S. *The Thoroughbred*. 4th ed. New York: Arco, 1971.

Moody, T.W., et al. *The Course of Irish History*. Lanham, MD: Roberts Rinehart Publishers, 2012.

Morris, Eric Andrew. "Horse Power to Horsepower: The External Costs of Transportation in the 19th Century City." Master's thesis, University of California, 2006.

Morris, Roy. *Lighting Out for the Territory: How Samuel Clemens Headed West and Became Mark Twain*. New York: Simon & Schuster, 2010.

Nasaw, David. *The Chief: The Life of William Randolph Hearst*. Boston: Houghton Mifflin, 2001.

National Archives and Records Administration. "Land Grands and Claims." Federal Court Records: Part 4. https://www.archives.gov/publications/ microfilm-catalogs/fed-courts/part-04.html.

Newbold, John D. "The Great California Flood of 1861–1862." *San Joaquin Historian* 5, no. 4 (Winter 1991).

Nichols, Jeffrey D. "Colonel Connor Filled a Varied, Dramatic Role in Utah." *History Blazer*, May 1995. https://historytogo.utah.gov/colonel-connor/.

Nickliss, Alexandra M. *Phoebe Apperson Hearst: A Life of Power and Politics.* Lincoln: University of Nebraska Press, 2018.

Nolan, Thomas P. "The Eureka Mining District, Nevada." Geological Survey Professional Paper 406. Washington, D.C.: United States Government Printing Office, 1962.

O'Farrell, P.A. *Butte: Its Copper Mines and Copper Kings.* New York: James A. Rogers, 1899.

O'Hanlon, Reverend J. *Irish Emigrant's Guide for the United States.* Boston: Patrick Donahoe, 1851.

Ó Murchadha, Ciarán. *The Great Famine: Ireland's Agony 1845–1852.* London: Bloomsbury Publishing, 2011.

Oxford University Press. *Oxford Reference.* https://www.oxfordreference.com.

Phelps, Alonzo. *Contemporary Biography of California's Representative Men.* San Francisco: A.L. Bancroft, 1881.

Philpott, Tom. "The Biblical Flood That Will Drown California." *Wired*, August 29, 2020.

Place, Marian T. *The Copper Kings of Montana.* New York: Random House, 1961.

Powell, Ada. *Copper, Green and Silver.* Hamilton, MT: A. Powell, 1993.

———. *Dalys of the Bitter Root.* Hamilton, MT: A. Powell, 1989.

Powers, Ron. *Mark Twain: A Life.* New York: Simon & Schuster, 2008.

Progressive Men of the State of Montana. Chicago: A.W. Bowen & Co., 1900.

Quivic, Frederick L. "Smoke and Tailings: An Environmental History of Copper Smelting Technologies in Montana, 1880–1930." PhD diss., University of Pennsylvania, 1998.

Rawls, James J., and Richard J. Orsi, eds. *A Golden State: Mining and Economic Development in Gold Rush California.* Berkeley: University of California Press, 1999.

Raymer, Robert G. "A History of Copper Mining in Montana." PhD diss., Northwestern University, 1929.

Reeve, W. Paul. "Father Lawrence Scanlan Established Catholic Church in Utah." *History Blazer*, September 1995.

Reilly, Gerry. "Montana Reunion 24th September 2008 Ireland." YouTube, August 2, 2020. https://www.youtube.com/watch?v=osrwaSODccc. Maureen Gill oral history, at 0:15:00–0:16:00, 0:19:00–0:22:00. (Cited as "Reilly video.")

Reilly, Gerry, and Mary Reilly. Email correspondence, December 5, 2021–June 3, 2022.

Rickard, Thomas A. *A History of American Mining*. A.I.M.E. Series. New York: McGraw Hill, 1932. Fourth Printing, York, PA: Maple Press, 1937.

Riordon, William L. *Plunkitt of Tammany Hall*. New York: McClure, Phillips, 1905.

Robbins, William G. "The Deconstruction of a Capitalist Patriarch: The Life and Times of Samuel T. Hauser." *Montana the Magazine of Western History* 42, no. 4 (Fall 1992): 20–33.

Robertson, William. *The History of Thoroughbred Racing in America*. New York: Bonanza Books/Prentice-Hall Publishers, 1964.

Rosenberg, Anna Fay. "Hard Winter Endurance: Conrad Kohrs' Cattle Raising Operation, 1887–1900." Master's thesis, University of Montana, 1996.

Ross, David. *Ireland: History of a Nation*. New Lanark, UK: Geddes & Grosset, 2002.

Rouse, Paul. *Sport and Ireland: A History*. Oxford, UK: Oxford University Press, 2015.

Sanders, Helen Fitzgerald. *A History of Montana*. Vol. 1. Chicago: Lewis Publishing Co., 1913.

Sergent, Amber Fogle. "The Pastime of Millions: James B. Haggin's Elmendorf Farm and the Commercialization of Pedigree Animal Breeding, 1897–1920." Master's thesis, University of Kentucky, 2012.

Shinn, Charles Howard. *The Story of the Mine: As Illustrated by the Great Comstock Lode of Nevada*. New York: D. Appleton and Co., 1897.

Shoebotham, H. Minar. *Anaconda: Life of Marcus Daly the Copper King*. Harrisburg, PA: Telegraph Press, 1956.

Sloan, Edward L. *Gazetteer of Utah and Directory of Salt Lake City*. Salt Lake City, UT: Salt Lake Herald Publishing, 1874.

Smith, Duane A. "Here's to Low-Grade Ore and Plenty of It, the Hearsts and the Homestake Mine." *Mining Engineering* vol. 55 no. 9, (September 2003): 10–14.

Smith, Grant H. *The History of the Comstock Lode, 1850–1920*. Reno: University of Nevada Bulletin, Nevada Bureau of Mines & Geology, 1943.

Smith, Ralph I. *History of the Early Reduction Plants of Butte, Montana*. Reprint, Butte: Montana School of Mines, 1953.

Svejda, George J. "Castle Garden as an Immigrant Depot, 1855–1890," National Park Service, U.S. Department of the Interior, December 2, 1968.

Swanberg, W.A. *Citizen Hearst*. New York: Charles Scribner's Sons, 1961.

Swibold, Dennis L. *Copper Chorus: Mining, Politics, and the Montana Press, 1889–1959*. Helena: Montana Historical Society Press, 2006.

Toole, K. Ross. "The Genesis of the Clark-Daly Feud." *Montana Magazine of Western History* 1, no. 2 (April 1951): 21–33.

———. "A History of the Anaconda Copper Mining Company: A Study in the Relationships Between a State and Its People and a Corporation, 1880–1950." PhD diss., University of California, 1954.

———. "Marcus Daly: A Study of Politics in Business." Master's thesis, University of Montana, 1948.

———. *Montana: An Uncommon Land*. 5th ed. Norman: University of Oklahoma Press, 1977.

Tullidge, Edward William. *The History of Salt Lake City and Its Founders.* Salt Lake City, UT: E.W. Tullidge, c. 1890.

Turnbull, Elsie. "Old Mines in the West Kootenay." *British Columbia Quarterly* 20, nos. 3–4 (July–October 1956): 147–64.

Twain, Mark. *Roughing It.* Hartford, CT: American Publishing Company, 1872. Project Gutenberg eBook, 2018.

United States Census Bureau. Decennial census. Department of Commerce. (Cited as "U.S. federal census [year].")

United States Congress. "Report of the Committee on Privileges and Elections of the United States Senate Relative to the Right and Title of William A. Clark to a Seat as Senator from the State of Montana, Vol 3." Vol. 1052 of the 56th Congress, 1st session 1899–1900. U.S. Government Printing Office, 1900. (Cited as "Senate testimony 1900.")

Utah History Encyclopedia. University of Utah Press, 1994. Online version, 1996. https://www.uen.org/utah_history_encyclopedia

Villanova University. "Fenian Brotherhood." Historic Papers. Digital Library at Villanova University. https://digital.library.villanova.edu.

Wahler, Brenda. *Montana Horse Racing: A History.* Charleston, SC: The History Press, 2019.

Weed, Walter Harvey. "Geology and Ore Deposits of the Butte District, Montana." Professional paper 74. U.S. Department of the Interior, USGS. Washington, D.C.: Government Printing Office, 1912.

Western Mining History. "Mining Town Archive." https://westernmininghistory. com/towns-archive/.

Whitehead, Bruce D., and Robert E. Rampton. "Bingham Canyon." In *From the Ground Up: The History of Mining in Utah*. Logan: Utah State University Press, 2006.

Whitley, Coleen K., ed. *From the Ground Up: The History of Mining in Utah.* Logan: Utah State University Press, 2006.

Woodham-Smith, Cecil. *The Great Hunger: Ireland 1845–1849.* 1st ed. New York: Harper and Row, 1962.

Workers of the Writers' Program, Writers' Project of Montana. *Copper Camp: The Lusty Story of Butte, Montana, the Richest Hill on Earth.* Missoula, MT: Riverbend Publishing, 1943. Reprint, 2001.

World Encyclopedia of Mythology. https://mythopedia.com. (Cited as "*Mythopedia*.")

Woulfe, Patrick. "*Irish Names and Surnames*, 1923." https://www.libraryireland.com/ names/contents.php.

Wrigley, Robert L. "Utah and Northern Railway Co.: A Brief History." *Oregon Historical Quarterly* 48, no. 3 (1947): 245–53.

Wyoming State Historical Society. https://www.wyohistory.org/index.

INDEX

ABOUT THE AUTHOR

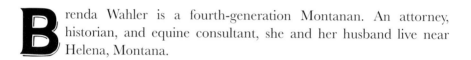

Brenda Wahler is a fourth-generation Montanan. An attorney, historian, and equine consultant, she and her husband live near Helena, Montana.